The 1865 Stoneman's Raid Ends

Joshua Beau Blackwell

The 1865 Stoneman's Raid Ends

Follow Him to the Ends of the Earth

The History Press

Published by The History Press
Charleston, SC 29403
www.historypress.net

Cover image: General Stoneman's Great Cavalry Raid, May 1863. *Courtesy of the Library of Congress.*

First published 2011

Manufactured in the United States

ISBN 978.1.60949.315.8

Library of Congress CIP data applied for.

To my parents:

I will get it together someday…

Contents

Preface

Staring out the sliver of double-paned glass that masqueraded as a classroom window, the end result of a misguided fiduciary measure that had blockaded a generation of inhabitants from the natural world, my back was turned toward two non-attentive student helpers. The feminine pair, who were plunging themselves headlong into the exhausting activity of dissecting the morning's hearsay, tore through more words at that particular moment than I had sighed in the preceding two months. No matter how hard I stroked my cowardly hairline in search of deliverance, the frivolous discussion continued to weigh heavy on an already exhausted mind.

Struggling in vain to ignore the typical banter of the youthfully enlightened, I found respite in the deep breath that filled my lungs, as well as the inevitable resonation of tar-saturated phlegm upon its exodus. Although perturbed at the auditory flagellation, my mind was otherwise fixated on a problem that I desperately wished not to confront. Staring at a line of rust-and-dust clunkers bathing in the early December morning's sun, a status symbol of the modern educator, the weight of my dilemma hit me with full force. With a longstanding obligation to The History Press nearing an end, I found myself in blatant violation of our contract.

An eternity ago, the middle weeks of June 2009 to be precise, a contact at The History Press haunted my phone in one fateful submission of ten numbers: those belonging to Doug Bostick. After as cordial a conversation as two strangers could hold in the anonymity of digital space, I was solicited to pen a brief study of the George Stoneman's Raid through the Carolinas. Hailing from a community that was affected by the campaign, I jumped at the offer. Without a stitch of previous research devoted to the topic, my hesitancy to commit to a lengthy study was expressed.

When it was brought to my attention that the company desired a book that was more narrative than academic, I began to relax at the task that confronted me. Thinking back to my freshman publication, "'Used to Be a Rough Place in them Hills': Moonshine, the Dark Corner and the New South," I was confident that I could mimic my efforts, and the wheels began to spin. Proposing the delivery of a piece that bordered just south of middle length in the time frame that they projected, the arrangement was sealed by the first day of July. As I delved into my task, however, I discovered just how very wrong I was.

The conundrum that presented itself that winter morning was not my inability to live up to the terms of the arrangement. In fact, my quandary was quite the opposite. What began as a late evening activity to unwind in the company of a few libations had devolved into an all-consuming effort to bring a much-neglected story of the American Civil War to life. By the time the most recent solstice had passed, the end result of this small book endeavor was beginning to resemble a tome.

Drawing a deep breath while thudding my head against a few of the bricks that encased the narrow window, I lamented the fact that I was legally obligated to dissect my yearlong efforts by two-thirds. Naturally, the dismemberment would completely ruin the memory of those whose folklore was being retold. Having researched and assembled the story for nearly sixteen months, I was almost certain that it would take half as long to deconstruct my efforts to its minimum.

As with many first-rate ideas, the inspiration for what unfolded was lost in the moment. I do not remember exactly what the spark was that prompted me to arrive at this conclusion, but not sparing any time, I politely asked the gossiping pair to quell their chitchat. Reaching for that same digital leash that had started this damned ordeal, I flipped through my contact list until I came across a number that I had dialed fewer times than the average person possessed fingers on any given hand. Doug Bostick, my commissioning editor.

Much to my surprise, and to his credit, this long-lost acquaintance answered within the first two rings—as I thought surely the unfamiliarity of my number would lead directly to voicemail limbo. Wasting no time on reintroductions, I informed my colleague that the book was complete and ready for submission two months ahead of schedule. The jovial nature of his voice, indicative of the complementary retort to the information, was dulled when I muttered the most feared quantifier that a messenger can espouse: "however." His momentary and contemplative silence was less uncomfortable than my elucidation. Explaining that I had written threefold what his company had desired, I stretched my luck and rolled the dice.

Expecting outright rejection, I was surprised to hear concurrence with my assumption that the endeavor would be done a disservice by abridgement. With the first hurdle cleared, the true test arrived. Swallowing hard, I proposed that the effort be divided into two distinct books that followed regional lines.

Agreeing that the first half of the raider's story could be concluded at the outskirts of Asheville, I was quite relieved to hear that Mr. Bostick was willing to take a chance on a book that expanded on the raid's progress through South Carolina. Long held as an accompanying sidebar to a footnote, the raiders' progress through the Palmetto State had largely been the realm of local United Daughters of the Confederacy chapters and was mostly absent from larger treatments of the war in the Carolinas. Much to my everlasting thanks, Doug was able to persuade The History Press to adopt my suggestions and provide the green light to finish the project properly.

The following work has been a true delight to produce. While the history of the American South has always been home to my academic curiosity, the true darling of my interest is the history of social conflict along the Blue Ridge of the Carolinas. Relishing yet another opportunity to broaden the topic through nonacademic narration, I find it pertinent to reiterate the entertaining nature of this work and its companion, *The 1865 Stoneman's Raid Begins: Leave Nothing for the Rebellion to Stand Upon*. As a firm believer in the merits of narrative history and oral tradition, only a cursory glance at any local library that stands along the path of the raid unveils a mammoth collection of recorded stories concerning both raider debauchery and civilian hardships. With such a large collection of stories, this book has given me the opportunity to engage in a style that I have long hoped to experiment with: the employment of a narrative license that micro history offers in order to explore a larger topic of study.

Fingerville, South Carolina
March 2011

Acknowledgements

Three books in as many years—needless to say, the end of the first decade of the twenty-first century has been inundated with work. My efforts, naturally, were not completed in a vacuum. In the previous two publications, I expressed thanks to those who have contributed to the final scribble clumsily disguised as a book. One continuous resident of the acknowledgement page, bedrock for all of my literary garble, needs to be brought to further light. She is Sarah Elizabeth Caldwell-Washburn.

This spectacular recipient of a hyphenated name, long the bane of those spawning from progressive pairings, has aided the development of my work well beyond what should be asked of a reasonable person. Resting at the heart of every attempt to refine the mountains of gibberish, ultimately distilling them into a coherent hill of prose, Sarah has been indispensable. Her understanding of grammar and uncanny eye for vocabulary missteps has shaped my literary style by proxy, giving the narration that fills my head a true voice on the page.

Although I hold an unsatisfied debt for her labors that can never truly be liquidated, I am monumentally more fortunate for pains undertaken beyond her skills as a wordsmith. Rocky and uneven, the long road of our turbulent friendship began at 7:34 p.m. on October 13, 2005. To this very day I cannot understand how the precise moment that our friendship was forged has remained entrenched in my head. Walking through the narrow hallway that divides the miniature dining room of Luther's in Beaufort, South Carolina, with the gigantic waterfront bar, I anxiously scanned the barroom for that evening's blind date. There she sat, third table along the wall; instantly, I knew that a new fixture had entered my life. Inseparable for the next six years, we laughed, cried, fought and loved, but always, it was her trust and support that I could rely on the most.

Since I have never been one to sport the moniker of emotionally stable, Sarah has stood as a rock for me this past half decade. However, time has taken a toll on our friendship. Much like water that fills the cracks of a boulder, freezes to ice and creates fissures that ultimately destroy it, the uneasiness that follows my company has worn her into apathy—a development for which I will loath myself for the remainder of my life. Now that our time is nearing an end, I can say without a shadow of a doubt that she has had a larger impact on my life than any other person that has ever crossed my path. Sarah, I am sorry for every stupid inconvenience that I have placed upon you, and best of luck to you in your future life.

Introduction

The World on Its Ear

Raw velocity, angelic in its invisibility, ruffled his sweat-sculpted mane unexpectedly. The corkscrew sensation that climbed out of the rider's loins and found refuge in his breast signified the return of an all-too-familiar feeling: the near impact of a one-ounce lead projectile. Instinctively jerking the reins of his malnourished half-caste to the left, the undesirable beast buckled its knees under the shattering jolt bestowed upon it. The end result was that equine and trooper plummeted toward the muddy road as one, and only avoided bone-pulverizing impact through the reflexes of the junior partner.

Juggling his carbine by the trigger guard while the mid-afternoon stillness was interrupted, the unnerved rider developed tunnel vision. As the air resonated with the sound of retorts, faulty percussion caps and a high-pitched harmony sung by flying projectiles, the detachment's head froze in place. Directing all of his senses toward the panicking hand that tried to position itself over the firing mechanism, the rattled trooper struggled to ready his weapon.

As he stabilized his unwieldy four-legged compatriot, rising plumes of smoke filled the horizon and betrayed the unseen assassins' locations. Finally mastering the long arm, he raised his bulky Enfield with a limb that pulsed with adrenaline and pulled the trigger. There was no answer. Understanding instantly his tragic folly, the rider drew the hammer out of the safety position and loosed a round into the quickly evaporating sulfur vapor.

Flooded with humiliated rage, the advance guard of Basil Dukes's cavalry column watched with aversion as a half dozen Union scouts broke the timber and made for the safety of the open pasture that lay beyond, knowing full well that their Confederate adversaries were unable to cut them down with empty barrels. Although the gray riders were momentarily out of danger and in control of the road that led toward Lincolnton, the infliction of a battered ego upon the unnerved sergeant superseded common sense. Solace could not be found in the fact that his men had responded to the surprise emergency with veteran expediency, as his own faltering had sullied what little pride remained in his soul after three years of hell. Still attempting to rein-in his shattered nerves following an amateur response to the inauguration of the engagement, deeply scarred pride sought to repair itself through bravado as the call to pursue bellowed from his throat no sooner than the sergeant had gathered his senses.

The moment of truth had arrived; his blood was up. As the Kentuckian cast a wild-eyed glance over his left shoulder, an adrenaline-saturated hand loosed its grip on the smoldering weapon, allowing his carbine to freely plummet to the end of its lanyard. Completely oblivious to the smoking muzzleloader's fate, the bluegrass Rebel reached across his body and securely fit his free hand onto the grip of a deeply worn saber. Unsheathing his metallic phallus, he bellowed, "Charge those bushwhacking bastards!" in an artificial baritone that did little to hide the fact that the sergeant was rattled to his core by an embarrassing display of reflexes. This romantic display of daring, truly an embodiment of antebellum cavalier spirit and a scene that was becoming all too rare in this late hour of the conflict, was swiftly betrayed by the most intelligent of Rebels to inhabit the roadway that particular noontime.

Confused at the suddenness of such a brazen order, the accompanying members of the advance guard responded to their sergeant's command without hesitation. Their mounts, however, had other opinions of this course of action. In line with the nature of the most intelligent of draft animals, these wily mules, which the princely riders of the South had degraded their station to mount in the name of necessity, refused to abide. Understanding the futile nature of the developments, many of the hybrids locked knee in a blatant refusal to waste their time pursuing the well-mounted Union raiders.[1]

Distraught at the betrayal, over two dozen spurs were pressed into the tender underbellies of the uncooperative animals—a futile effort with which to inspire patriotism. Hailing from a region that was not entirely unfamiliar with the intricacies of back-busting farm labor, many of the riders were not naive to the nature of their mounts. Drawing tightly upon the reins, the sergeant dusted off bellows that had remained idle in his repertoire for the previous three years. Although the old mainstay of "Yaa!" was drawn at the first sign of refusal, as it had been while proudly resting on more palatable mounts under more favorable circumstances, the direness of the pursuit called for more ornate measures.[2]

Reverting to his years behind the plow, the young noncommissioned officer let loose with agrarian vernacular in an attempt to move his stubborn mount in any direction. Flapping the left rein frantically in an effort to induce any movement whatsoever, rustic bellows filled the panicky air: "Haw! Haw!" Naturally, the yeoman lingo sounded across the roadway to no avail. Not to be outdone, the right rein was slapped against the beast while its counterpart was drawn taut and the ensuing "Gee! Gee!" echoed through the erect ears of the unwieldy draft. Overcome with desperation, frantic emotion began to surface. "Goddamn your eyes—just do something!" The embattled sergeant's experiences were not exclusive. Averting his eyes from the chestnut hide of his uncooperative partner, he could see that every one of his troopers was reduced to bargaining with the cumbersome animals.

With the mules growing impatient with the rude behavior of their reckless riders, the disagreement escalated. Under the constant barrage of spur thrust, which was beginning to puncture the hide of some of the burdened

With the command stretched throughout the upstate of South Carolina, the criminal elements began to skulk away and engage in open banditry, outfitting themselves as best they could on what their fortunes afforded them. *Courtesy of the Library of Congress.*

laborers, the beasts threw several of the overzealous cavalrymen from the saddle. Of particular note was the sergeant, whose eyes readjusted to the world just in time to witness a pair of chestnut haunches galloping in the opposite direction. As the realization settled in that the laurels of the day's action were not to rest upon his head, lament took over: "Son-of-a-bitch!"

The pursuit was a comedy of errors, and after a few minutes elapsed, the sergeant was dissuaded from his attempts at redemption. The moment had passed, and the fleeing raiders were most likely regrouping with their company-level companions. Sticking out like sore thumbs as frozen silhouettes along an open horizon, some action had to be taken to improve the detachment's station. With no other alternative than dismounting, the detachment abandoned its advancement to the unseen confines of the tree line that the Union raiders had abandoned and began to hastily walk their mounts back toward Morganton lest the Union troopers return to exploit the Confederates' vulnerable state.

While the majority of his men were dismounting and leading their four-legged saviors mulishly back to the confines of safety, the shucked members of the detachment engaged in a coaxing test of will with their former mounts. Taking advantage of the lull to entice his agitated mount back to within arm's length, the bruised helmsman commenced to plow furrows down the shoulder of the road with the hooves of his obstinate counterpart. This demonstration in mutual stubbornness, a result of sheer determination

Although a jovial learning experience, these St. Patrick's Day revelers in a Union camp were introduced to a constant that others had to learn under combat conditions: the uncooperative disadvantages of using mules as cavalry mounts. *Courtesy of the Library of Congress.*

to dominate the other, continued for some length until the party was met by a courier. The orders were expected: establish a picket line along the road and hold it until relieved.

Understanding that picket duty had the potential to transform into an unpleasantly long tenure, the detachment collectively agreed to secure as many creature comforts as its station could afford. After dispatching two riders, whose sole qualifications were their possession of the cadre's most tenable mounts, little under an hour had elapsed before one of the scouts returned with delightfully unexpected news. After cautiously advancing a few hundred yards beyond the site of the ambush, it was discovered that a suitable homestead lay just off the roadside. Coming to the realization that the Union scouts had likely taken up residence in the most palatial lodging that the area had to offer, the sergeant instructed his detachment to mount up and cautiously advance back to its original place of shame.

In short order, the detachment was reunited as it came across an impatient private embedded in the very brambles that had secreted the bushwhackers less than two hours earlier. Expressing distaste for the half hour of isolation spent in inhospitable country through the gruff nature of his delivery, it was quickly pointed out that the farmhouse was inhabited by a small collection of local women; although children were present, no men were to be found. "They were certainly here to stay the afternoon," the scout proclaimed with some authority. "One of the ladies walked up to me a few minutes before y'all arrived, said that they had been here all morning and had pretty much picked them clean." Continuing on in disgust, he added, "She's been asking if we got anything to spare them."

Having expected such a parasitic request, the sergeant continued in an elevated boast, "Hell, I was about to ask them the same in turn." The joke was not lost on his troopers, as a few cynical chuckles rolled out of the dust-covered crowd. Delegating responsibility in the establishment of a bivouac and a proper ambush, the sergeant turned to the lone sentry and requested a formal introduction to the inhabitants of their newfound abode.

The walk across the yard was a beeline and absent the ornate small talk that is usually bred out of uncomfortable silence. While his guide studied the early spring dust that was rising as his feet shuttled through the dry patches of the property's scratch yard, the sergeant surveyed the spread for any potential opportunity—a clear sign that his recent habits had quickly taken hold of his subconscious. Ascending the stairs of a porch cluttered with farm implements brought closer to earshot for safekeeping in the night, he was disappointed to find that there was no sign of movement in the nearby barn, a sign that the previous visitors had gone through the property relieving it of livestock and, most likely, any objects of value inside the house.

The door swung ajar before the pair could announce their presence, as the nervous inhabitants had carefully watched their approach. Frail, but unwavering, the spokeswoman for the collection of gaunt females and narrow children who resided within was a middle-aged woman who had unfortunately gone gray long before her time. The dress she sported was periodically crowned with patches, a clear sign that her clan had fallen upon hard times. Yet the reserved necessity for the employment of her skills as a seamstress signified that the inhabitants were not in dire straits—the first fortunate development to have befallen the sergeant that day.

Invitation inside was not only unspoken but also customarily expected considering the mild solace taken from the drab color of the pair's garments. Crossing an unattended threshold, a subtle cursory glance had to suffice as substitute for a thorough survey of the dwelling and its inhabitants. The room, obviously pilfered by its previous visitors, was filled with four other women and a few children, although the sounds of whispered conversation in adjoining rooms and the groan of the ceiling joist under transitive weight indicated that there were other hidden inhabitants at points throughout the house.

Unaware of what pitfalls he was blinded to, the sergeant elected to continue his duty instead of engaging in mischief from the onset. Not mincing words, the sergeant got straight to the point, "How long was that squad here, and how many of them were they?" The unannounced inquisition took the woman aback and raised the heads of most of the inhabitants scattered about the room.

Bathed in warm relief, the welcoming mood of the host and cordial tone of the conversation changed almost instantly as a malevolent sneer crept across the lips of the senior-most trooper in the room. Pressing the issue by nursing an artificial slight, the sergeant chided, "We rode right up on those Yankees." Cultivating tension, the elder rider turned directly to the mute inhabitants who lined two of the walls of the room: "Why in the hell did you all not sound out? One of my boys could have been killed, for Christ's sake!"

Artificial rage hallooed through his throat. "But I guess a gaggle of unionist whores such as you wouldn't think twice about allowing those bastards to cut us down without the common courtesy to announce their presence!" Every adult eye in the room, discounting the troopers who had been through this charade more times than they cared to remember, widened with the sudden accusation, leaving a half dozen heads shaking in panicky disbelief. Stepping forward to defend her station, the matron of the house sounded her protest, "Wait! You don't under—"

The plea was cut short by the abrupt snap of a lofted backhand. "Hold your tongue woman!" It was an insulting order that had its full effect, as the sheer terror that radiated from her eyes was indication enough that the spokeswoman had recanted her objection—an apology further made evident by the immediate retreat from her aggressive stance. Coming to the realization that the situation was rapidly deteriorating, the matron attempted to validate the party's silence during the occupation of the farmstead. Unwilling to entertain any explanatory countermeasures, indicative of the second step in the detachment's well-oiled con, the trooper's ruse followed its prescribed path without deviation. "Enough belly crawling woman," he said. "How are you and yours set for provisions?"[3]

Stuttering in response to the unexpected query, the woman nervously provided a scant inventory from memory. Prodding his latest victim as to the cache's location, the woman led her inquisitor upstairs while the silent private nonchalantly covered his superior's only avenue of escape by leaning against the starting newel. Scaling a narrowly enclosed elliptical staircase, the conditionally chaste sergeant was transfixed by his chaperone's slender frame as her lean buttocks tauntingly danced underneath the obstructive homespun garment. But it was her nervous right hand that garnered the most attention. Trembling to an extent that the uncontrollable quiver caused disconnect with the handrail as the pair crested the second floor, a nervous whimper filled the adjoining hallway. "Margaret, I have a solider visitor with me, and he wants to see the board."

Frozen in place, the unseen inhabitants of the second floor left the upstairs void of sound. After an uncomfortably long pause, a muffled retort echoed from one of the bedrooms. "Hold for a moment, will ya. Joanna isn't decent." Turning slightly to her rear and raising her left arm, the hostess intuitively informed the sergeant that it would be just a moment before entry would be granted to the occupied room. In a moment, the signal was howled for the pair to enter. Following his increasingly suspicious victim, the trooper was welcomed by the sight of a woman lying on a bed in one corner of the room while an attendant hastily removed nails from a series of floorboards to reveal a cavity.

The exposed nook was filled to the brim with sacks of cornmeal, numerous strands of leather britches and a salted ham—roughly in the same quantity that the reluctant hostess had confessed to just a few moments earlier. The conditional bandit, however, was too keen of a birddog to be thrown by the attempted hoax. Unleashing a heartfelt sigh at the prospect of his visitation turning ugly, the sergeant lamented, "That is a scant collection of victuals to sustain such a large coop of hens."

Turning his attention to the bed-bound woman, a fair-skinned adolescent of medium stature, it was brought to his attention by the guide that she had been moved to the upper story of the dwelling after succumbing to a fever. Noticing a single-barrel shotgun resting on a wall within grasp of the bedridden teenager, the trooper casually slid his hand over his holster and passively slid the leather clasp from its home, exposing the pistol's grip. With polished walnut touching flesh, the sergeant demonstrated his very observant eye. "Why is that fever-laden woman next to a shotgun?" He followed his rhetorical question with a damning observation: "She looks awfully flush for an infected cockchafer." Any bravado that the planted sentinel may have harbored dissipated as she knew the jig was up.

Surveying the pile of blankets that she rested her faux illness upon, the trooper instantly noticed the intermittent creases throughout the bed. Clearing his throat as an extra measure to express his authority over the room, he mused, "What if we were to say you get your ass off of that stockpile there and pull them blankets to one side?" Reluctantly repositioning herself on the bed, a muted protest in hopes that the con could be salvaged, the young woman slowly rose to a sitting position on the shrouded secret. Forcing eye contact upon her unexpected guest, hate conjuring an icy glare that could freeze water, the youth reached across the length of the cache and pulled the farthest corner to her with a defiant jerk. The message behind the demonstration was not lost on the trooper.

"You're quite a firebrand," jested the sergeant. "If you were just a little riper, I might have to pluck your cherry myself." Slowly inching toward the uncovered windfall, the outnumbered bandit positioned his back against the wall in hopes that he might avoid waylay from any of the three hellions that surrounded him.

Quickly turning his attention to the horde, it was evident that his suspicions of the caloric solvency of the clan were correct. Biting down on the inside flesh of his lip so as to not smile at the misfortune that his detachment was about to impose on the fairer sex of the farm, he bellowed out, "Jessie, call out for a couple more to come up here, and tell them to bring some saddle bags!" The commotion rising up from the first floor was all that the sergeant needed to arrive at the understanding that the deed was underway and that his men would have provisions for the next week or so.

Reestablishing eye contact with the room's other inhabitants, he was overcome with compulsion to express an adequate apology for the events that were about to unfold. "Ladies, I'm sorry, but they aren't sending us a damn stitch of supplies." He continued with his halfhearted explanation, "Every goddamn trooper west of Raleigh is going to be coming down that road in the next few hours, so if it isn't my boys who are going to relieve you of it, then someone else will." The words were lost on the freshly minted victims; the old matron was shocked, the keeper of the decoy did nothing but stare at her feet in ashamed failure and the teenage hellion shook in barely containable rage.

In no time, the room was swarming with troopers, as four members of the detachment had answered the call to pilfer the home. Resigned to provide for his accompaniment yet also demonstrate a token of leniency toward his victims, the sergeant prescribed what quantities of the rations were to be lifted. No sooner had his men begun to reduce the store into a disheveled pile than sounds of distress rolled up the stairwell from the first floor, letting it be known that at least one of his men was searching the lower-level inhabitants for any trinket of value that might have been left by the Federal raiders the previous hour. Instructing his subordinates to leave the decoy unmolested as they brought their harvest to a close, he abandoned the tragic scene in an effort to examine the nature of the commotion downstairs.

Descending the final few stairs of the enclosed staircase, an expected sight befell his eyes. There, in the sitting room of the first floor, the remaining inhabitants of the dwelling were lined up against a wall. Tears streamed down the collection of young and old faces as a private from the detachment was ransacking random drawers of a cabinet that occupied the space of a nearby corner. Examining the distraught confusion that was harbored in many of the faces, it was clear that the trooper had already inspected their personages with no success; he was now frantically attempting to uncover any acumen whatsoever from hidden spots within the homestead.

"Private," sounded the sergeant, "I doubt there is anything here worth looking for." Ignoring the notion, the private moved to another point in the room and drew a knife to dissect the cushion of a chair. Not to be ignored or to visit any unneeded destruction upon his captives, the ranking Confederate in the room sounded off: "Boy, I said it's useless, and you best sheath that knife."

This degrading quantifier, best reserved for bonded servants, had its attention-getting effect. Injured yet unmoved, his retort was swift: "To hell with you!" The insolent reply was greeted by the sounds of blue metal swiping well-tanned leather and the mechanical hallmarks of a hammer drawn to the firing position.

Yet another in a long line of moments of truth, this test of wills lacked the hallmarks of weakness that his men had tested in previous weeks. "Private, I'm not suggesting, I'm telling you that there is nothing for you here." Resisting the temptation to take aim into the back of his frozen subordinate, the sergeant continued, "I think it's best if you just wait outside for the others." Not trying his luck, the private sighed as he returned his straight blade to its holster and submissively turned for the front door in an effort to avoid the determined eyes of his superior.

With the crisis averted, the sergeant began to apologize to the lower-floor inhabitants for their inconvenience, although no mention was made of the life-giving provisions that his men were extorting from the gaggle with light fingers. Halfway through the monotonous and ill-formed apology, the remainder of the invaders trickled downstairs. Glinting eyes, primitive in their signal, was the only indication needed to relay that adequate provender was in their possession. Turning his attention away from an apathetic apology, the sergeant inquired, "What did you do with the remainder?" Informed that the faux floorboards had been stuffed to the brim with the thoroughly combed remnants, a silent nod by the chief of the marauders was all that was needed to demonstrate his satisfaction.

Knowing full well that the afternoon's developments had been fruitful was all that spun through the sergeant's mind as his malevolent cavalcade crossed the yard. Upon pressing one of his privates, the contents of the haul were conveyed to him. As the inventory rang through his ears—dried vegetables, cornmeal, ham and numerous preserved delicacies—it became clear that his men would go without want for the remainder of the war's late-hour fiascos. Upon returning to the picket line, the ill-gotten gains were distributed amongst the men.

It was at that moment that the unpleasant feeling returned. Rising deep from within his stomach, a queer sensation—akin to the conscientious sting that burns the souls of adulterers when faced with their unsuspecting spouses in the wake of infidelity—began to take hold of the ranking trooper. Disgusted with himself and his proximity to his latest victims, the sergeant ordered the detail to mount up and withdraw from the property, an exodus undertaken in hopes of nursing his shame in the shade of another tree-lined pasture.

The monotonous creak of an oscillating saddle kept his ears entertained as the detachment retreated a quarter mile down the road. Although the fullest extent of his concentration was committed to the metered friction of tanned leather, only the lament of leaving yet another tiny piece of his soul with the women in exchange for the last of their provisions filled his mind. Cresting the tree line to the pasture in which the riders had been ambushed just two hours earlier, he mused that perhaps this latest affront was the last time—surely it was the last time.

THE EXPLOITATION OF civilians by both Northern and Southern combatants along the roads that led to Asheville from Salisbury was just another tragic scene in the late-war raid that had been rapidly advancing through western North Carolina and southwestern Virginia. By the time the cavalry division under George Stoneman had completed its task of rendering Salisbury, North Carolina, useless to the remaining Confederates, the discipline of both warring armies in the upland Carolinas had greatly deteriorated. Increasingly, self-preservation superseded discipline as the final moments of the war ticked away.[4]

Having waged war for the better part of four years, the troopers of both sides were coming to the realization that the conflict was rapidly coming to an end. As with any population, there was a large contingency that migrated away from the call of duty and began to hunt out an avenue for self-gain—be it what they saw as reimbursement for their troubles or a need to establish a security net for the hardships they knew would come from living in a conquered land. Naturally, the sting of falling victim to both armies' combatants, with no trustworthy provider of the rule of law to be found, had on impact on the psyche of the noncombatants of the region. The end result were myriad stories about the depredations that armed combatants inflicted on countless families who lay in the path of the campaign. Contrary to popular belief, as the war drew to a close, the color of the uniform mattered little.[5]

Striking out of Knoxville, Tennessee, on March 21, 1865, the cavalry division under George Stoneman had been instrumental in bringing a conclusion to the war in Southern Appalachia. Destroying infrastructure throughout western North Carolina, the raiders had penetrated southwestern Virginia by April 3. It was there that their laundry list of destruction rendered the seldom-assaulted region useless to the dying Confederacy. Widely fragmented and actively engaged throughout the hills surrounding Lynchburg, Virginia, the confusion created by the division's presence in the Army of Northern Virginia's rear directly led to its commander, Robert E. Lee, declaring his situation hopeless and seeking terms with Ulysses S. Grant.[6]

Excusing himself from the field due to an embarrassingly crippling ailment following the destruction of the Confederate infrastructure at Salisbury, George Stoneman was largely derelict in his leadership via proxy as his division wound its way through the North Carolina mountains and into the upstate of South Carolina. *Courtesy of the Library of Congress.*

Reentering western North Carolina without understanding the impact they had on bringing the war in Virginia to a close, the raiders struck out for Salisbury, North Carolina, home to one of the last major prisons in the Confederacy. Although the liberation of the prison was bittersweet due to the fact that the stockades were empty by the time the raiders captured them—the entire prison having been emptied through diplomatic bargaining just a few weeks earlier—its destruction and the incineration of the large military stores found in the city had a major impact on the continuation of the conflict in North Carolina. With the vital Confederate infrastructure in Salisbury reduced to ashes, the definition of the raid began to transform from the fast-paced life of rear-echelon destructors into the monotony of an occupying army.[7]

By the time April was in full bloom, the men under George Stoneman's command were beginning to divide themselves into smaller fragments with the intention of occupying western North Carolina in order to curtail any possibility of a guerrilla war developing in the region. Then there was the

This 1863 lithograph greatly exaggerated any success that the 1865 raid's namesake, George Stoneman, had in his aborted expedition toward Richmond during the Chancellorsville Campaign. *Courtesy of the Library of Congress.*

In the summer of 1863, George Stoneman led the largest cavalry operation of the War into the rear of Robert E. Lee's Army of Northern Virginia during the Chancellorsville Campaign. However, like many of his other grand disasters, the elements sabotaged his efforts. Here, his division sits idle waiting for the flood to subside at Kelly's Ford, Virginia. *Courtesy of the Library of Congress.*

In a lightly veiled attempt to celebrate the menial accomplishments of the embattled commander, this illustration was released to the public shortly after Stoneman's lukewarm performance during the Chancellorsville Campaign in 1863. *Courtesy of the Library of Congress.*

By the time East Tennessee native Alvan Gillem departed from Salisbury, his dual notorieties as bloodthirsty warmonger and Unionist hero were well entrenched among his respective observers. It was his misstep at Asheville, however, that tipped the scale toward the former for many throughout the region. *Courtesy of the Library of Congress.*

commander himself. Stuck lame by a long-standing infirmary—exaggerated hemorrhoids—Stoneman made the decision to return to Tennessee after his command dusted the streets of Statesville and leave the destiny of his charge in the hands of Alvan Gillem, a loyalist from East Tennessee, who had long ago developed a propensity for extracting revenge against the rebellious classes of the Secessionist South.[8]

Gillem was not alone, as many of the raid's members were locals who had sided with the Union cause, colloquially known as "Home Yankees." The notorious Third Brigade, composed of riders who sought revenge for the ills placed on their families by the Confederate government, fell under the command of a former Tennessee sheriff by the name of John Miller. Although his actions and motives varied little from the overzealous "Home Yankees" found under Miller's command, the mixture of native-born and Northern troopers who served in Simon B. Brown's Second Brigade were just as reckless and destructive. Although very astute in the execution of his duty, in the end, it was this alderman hailing from St. Claire, Michigan, who inflicted the most harm on civilians.[9]

Even though the discipline, morale and devotion to duty of the Second and Third Brigades rapidly eroded as the command returned to the mountains of western North Carolina, there was a stalwart of restraint amongst the pack of wolves. William Jackson Palmer, originally from Leipzig, Delaware, but receiving a commission in Pennsylvania due to his ties with the local railroad industry, was the last remaining harbor of discipline by the time the raid had completed its mission. Diligent in his duty and constantly aware that his subordinate commanders were losing control of their men, his late raid story became that of one pissing into the wind—constantly maintaining the high level of discipline that he had come to expect from his First Brigade while trying to instill any semblance of discipline in the two wayward sister brigades.[10]

Although initially successfully in their efforts to bring the rebellion to a close, the well-disciplined riders of Stoneman's Raid quickly devolved into marauders. By the time the month of May was over, no other command in the American Civil War had experienced a decline in discipline, purpose or morale that could rival the one experienced by those attached to the name of George Stoneman Jr. As the command entered Georgia, by way of upstate South Carolina, thousands of mounted individuals were essentially nothing more than a well-organized mob of bandits—save the efforts to restore discipline at the hand of General Palmer.[11]

The end result was a plethora of offenses toward civilians, government property and the few holdings of the emancipated that the collective memory of the region has long remembered. Although many of the members were vindictive toward the planter class—not out of opportunism but due to the desire to level the social playing field against many of those who had wronged their families in the years leading up to the raid—the undertones of social justice are lost in the gross misbehavior of the raid's participants. As the degree of debauchery mounted, commitment to the Union war effort became practically nonexistent. In the end, it was perhaps the feverous pursuit of the renegade president Jefferson Davis and the mythical icon of the Confederate treasury that salvaged any good in the raid's reputation once it departed North Carolina.

1
"False to Their God and Traitors to Their County"

Fast!" The irritatingly sharp ring of the word carved through the stagnant afternoon air generating a patience-shattering effect that is all but foreign to those unaccustomed to monosyllabic commands. "Faster, we must dig faster!" The young men who scratched away at the rocky red soil of the Cherokee foothills were nearing completion of an emergency excavation that was biblical in scale. The wiry old man who was aiding the frantically diligent workers by cascading the obvious upon them, as if the slogans espoused from his jowls were indispensable directives, was given the birth name Logan Carson. To Carson, however, it was more agreeable to his demeanor to address him by the self-given moniker of "colonel," although his military heritage was slightly north of dubious. Pacing like a jackal over a hole that one observer reminisced was large enough to have concealed a piano, Carson was noticeably consumed by wrenched nerves, knowing that the notorious body of raiders was rapidly approaching via a stagecoach road that dissected his property as it snaked its way to Asheville.[12]

These two excavators, slender and white, with sun-tarnished skin, who had somehow managed to avoid the Confederate draft or convinced the local powers that they were indispensable to the homefront, were approached by Carson due to the one unequaled quality that they possessed as manual laborers at this midnight hour of the conflict: their skin color. Knowing full well that the self-anointed senior officer had problems with human property, his slaves having earlier gone so far as to betray the old man's identity to unknown riders in an effort to facilitate his capture, Carson suspected that had the plantation's black males been entrusted with the cache, they would have been all too eager to divulge its resting place once the Union raiders inquired of its location. Understanding that his hirelings were more than capable of completing the task at hand, the aging colonel knelt down, placing his hand on a spade, and asked his niece to accompany him into the forest behind the main house as he thrust a small linen-wrapped bundle into her milky white hands.[13]

Excruciating for his weathered years, the heart-pounding pace was exhausting. Hurdling ancient water oak roots, passing his arms through tacky cedar limbs and forcing his battered knees through the ascent of practically impassable laurel thickets, the old man led his young female pack mule toward their destination. "Here, this is the spot." The satisfaction of the revelation rested on his shoulders like a warm blanket and alleviated the tension cramp that clenched within his arches after a dozen or so minutes of walking through the moist, dark soil that crowned the terrain of the forest. Filling his lungs with a deep sigh of satisfaction, a relieved exhale muddled his pacified lament: "This must be the spot. It will never cross their heathen minds to come this far."

Intermittent daylight created a foreboding landscape that unnerved even the most weathered of mountaineers. Roots, which sent countless fingers jutting deep into the iron-stained mountain soil, broke the horizon and snaked along their course until once again submerging into the rolling terrain. As the afternoon sun became disoriented in the thick canopy of the eastern Appalachian forest, the bark-covered obstacles breathing in the open air took on the appearance of logs bowing before the soil as it capitulated to the earthy deep. As the glistening sunlight saturated the fragrant April breeze, the colonel placed the tip of his iron spade at the base of a root-encrusted bank and pressed firmly with his foot against the foundation of the implement. As the wafts of odorous particles generated by the disturbed earthy topsoil filled his nostrils, the old gentleman knew that his cache would be safe at last.

The hole that was carved out in the peculiar soil was distinctly remembered by the aging paternalist's niece. Less than a foot long, half as wide, as well as deep, the minor slit was not of the magnitude of the canyon that was being completed just a few hundred yards away, but the contents of the grave were exponentially greater in value. While salt-cured winter hams were being stacked one on the other like cordwood in the summertime and the piano-sized cavern swelled with occupants, the faltering folding money that embodied the renegade investments of the colonel was neatly tucked inside the narrow sliver, finally entombed from the tempered hands of the

Federal picklocks by the efforts of his iron spade. Following the concealment of the worthless Confederate scrip that marked his collapsing fortune, a few handfuls of bark kissed by the sweet aroma of southern Appalachian moss were scraped from the north side of neighboring trees and strategically piled atop of the freshly turned dirt.[14]

"Dear lord, please!" Staring at his earth-stained hands, which had just that very moment completed a cementation of the emerald green thatch upon the broken ground, the schizophrenic appeals of a troubled soul resonated in the darkness: "Please, I have always been a loyal servant—spare my hearth from the Babylonians." Rising from his decrepit knees, the old man turned and began to retrace his steps to his plantation home without summoning his niece. Lumbering through the old growth of the groves, alone in his thoughts, the old man attempted to dissect any contingency in his wrecked mind. "They will search the house, yet I suspect that they are on a time table, a schedule that will not take kindly to the hardships imposed upon delay. They won't search the grounds; there is not enough time to comb the grounds." His thoughts were queerly interrupted by a unique hum in the distance—the sounds of men engaging in the desperate struggle of life or death on the horizon.

Upon returning to the manorial grounds, it became all too apparent that his foresight was well founded. With the rumbling sounds of skirmishing in the distance filling the spirals of his ears, Carson stared at the fresh earth slathered where the massive cavern used to be and instantly knew that without garnish, the ruse would be a wasted effort. Without delay, the quick-thinking colonel ordered the refuse from his property strewn over the ground. Following the completion of the dilapidated heap, the monument to the wastefulness of man was topped with pine straw and fallen leaves to complete the illusion. Inspecting his earthen masquerade like a painter perusing a well-invested canvas, the only thought that gamboled through the old man's mind was that with any luck, his efforts would pay off.[15]

Typical of strategies utilized by the social hierarchy of western North Carolina, the forlorn actions taken by the Carson family were the only aesthetics of security that could be mustered as the Home Yankee column under General Gillem made its return trip toward the ominous spires of the Blue Ridge. Although the plantation's stock of hams was secured and a cache of paper-thin Confederate currency was abandoned to rot in the company of the forest roots, the house itself became an inviting beacon of pilferage that drew the troopers to it like moths to a flame. Although long in the tooth for an opportunity to further stuff the embossed saddlebags that draped from the sides of their mounts, their approach was inconveniently slower than the enterprising troopers would have liked. The agitating blister that impeded an otherwise serene ride through the hill country was a handful of local infantrymen who intended to defend their homes from the same fate that had befallen Salisbury.

The engagement that echoed through the ears of the Carson family was the result of a simple reconnoiter by components of a brigade of infantry that had taken up residence in Asheville under the auspices of General James Green Martin. As the ragtag Confederate infantry withdrew along the cut of a creek bank in skirmish formation, a courier riding past the Carson House informed the colonel of the developments that were transpiring a mere mile away. Aside from the traumatizing information that a skirmish was being conducted along his property line, the owner of the freshly christened battlefield was also informed that the blue riders slowly ebbing toward his doorstep were rounding up any adult males they could place their hands on and kidnapping them under the false pretense of prisoners of war.[16]

Understanding that the burden imposed on his aging body by a long uphill forced march into loyalist Tennessee would amount to nothing less than a death sentence, Carson heeded the advice of the rider and the pleas of his family to vacate his holding. Tethering his precious draft animals to his mount, the old man procured enough victuals to satisfy his appetite for the duration of his exile and led the train of animals into the surrounding hillsides in a desperate search for reprieve from an exhaustive demise. No sooner had the patriarch retreated from his kingdom than the dreaded blue riders came into view of the abandoned family. The dusty column rapidly advanced along the stagecoach road toward Marion in hopes of circumventing a possible Confederate rally near the village's outskirts.[17]

The first squad that arrived on the property was all business and only demanded to know the whereabouts of the family's livestock. To their request, the stalwart Mrs. Carson lied that their chattel hands had taken them down the road in an attempt to keep them from the hands of the raiders. Falling for the ploy, the advance guard continued its course along the road. However, any sigh of relief that could have been breathed was ill timed. Within a matter of minutes, several companies arrived on the property, bearing the same unrelenting questions. This collection of troopers did not follow their brethren on to Marion, electing to instead bivouac in the yard that surrounded the main house. In spite of the isolation from friendly males, as all of the free and bonded men had vacated the property, the women of the Carson family made it through the evening unmolested.[18]

With the sun resuming its daily course on the morning of April 18, General Gillem arrived on site ill-tempered and famished. Barging into the Carson home, Gillem demanded of the reluctant host that he and his staff be fed at their expense. Understanding that the skills cultivated over the decades spent mastering the role of plantation matron left her with major inadequacies in culinary ability, the aging wife of Colonel Carson insisted that this request was impossible as her cooks had all run off after first word of the troopers' presence in the region. The dilemma was of no concern to the cantankerous general, as he insisted that the blueblood remove herself from his presence in an effort to prepare the meal with her callus-free hands or his men would be turned loose on the house without restraint.[19]

Collapsing in the face of the threat, Mrs. Carson dutifully prepared subpar fare for Gillem and his closest officers. Understandably taken aback by the bland biscuits, whose only seasoning was the charred encasement that held back a still miry flour and water porridge, the dissatisfied general followed through with his threat even though the matron of the house had given an honest effort to pacify his hunger. Opening the door and leaving it ajar as a signal to his more daring wolves, Gillem left the property, bound for Marion. What followed was an unsightly, masterful demonstration in the science of vandalism that has been seldom repeated.[20]

Not wasting any time, the more brazen riders entered the home uninvited, corralled the defenseless women and sequestered them in the very dining room their commanding officer had just abandoned. The ferocity of the ransacking was monumental, as not a single drawer or trunk was left undisturbed. While the house was being turned upon its ear in search of traditional loot, a chaos-induced frenzy resulted in many family valuables of no monetary value being either pilfered or destroyed. A purloined item of particular disbelief to the women was the property of a centennial slave by the name of Aunt Lucindy.[21]

Unimposing as any ragged scrap of cloth, a shawl that had been passed down to her by a provenience long forgotten had been stored in a trunk in an upstairs bedroom in an effort to protect it from moths. Perhaps for no other motivation than sure meanness, the ancient shawl, having only accrued sentimental value, was draped over a trooper's shoulders as he vacated the house. Following the burglary of every valuable worth carting away from the home, a keg of molasses was brought from a storehouse. Placed in the front sitting room, the barrel was tilted on its side, and a swift axe blow drove the bung into the barrel. Afterward, two troopers lifted the barrel and began to maliciously pour its contents over all of the furniture and carpeting they could cover until the sticky extract was completely expended.[22]

Stopping along the stagecoach road on the outskirts to Marion to rest his mount, Gillem received the unexpected news that organized Confederate resistance was still to be found in the region of western North Carolina. While the Federal advanced guard reported to the increasingly twisted general that the Swannanoa Gap was being heavily fortified, General James Green Martin was desperately consolidating all the available forces in the southeastern mountains of North Carolina and erecting fortifications east of Asheville. Moving a brigade of infantry and artillery under Confederate general John B. Palmer into the steeply inclined roadway, the busted backs of the entrenching command were augmented by Robert Love's sizeable battalion from William Holland Thomas's famous legion of mountaineers and Cherokee Indians. The fortifications were unprecedented for the mountains, and upon receiving reports from his scouts concerning these unexpected developments, Gillem called for a council to reassess the raiders' course into the city of Asheville.[23]

Faced with the unacceptable prospect of a full frontal assault against a well-entrenched veteran infantry during what could very well be the last week of the war, Gillem set his mind to work. The strategy that sprung

Originally hailing from eastern North Carolina, James Martin was appalled by the treatment of his adoptive Asheville at the hands of the Second and Third Brigades. *Courtesy of the Library of Congress.*

from the old Tennessean's brain was an elaborate cavalry march along the right flank of the Confederates that would take his saddle-weary troopers over fifty miles out of the way in a protracted hook around their enemy's devilishly fortified position. Knowing full well that the Confederates were more concerned with the problems presented by the presence of loyalist mountaineers than they were with enemy combatants originating from the North, the conniving general took advantage of the defenders' fears. Leaving the Third Brigade in front of the defenses at Swannanoa Gap, the Confederates would have their hands full, as John K. Miller was instructed to probe the works, feint throughout the various gaps of the region and be aggressive with the isolated homes along the surrounding ridges in an attempt to dislodge the entrenched Confederates without pushing a general engagement. While Miller was conducting this deadly ballet just a few miles east of Asheville, Gillem would take the Second Brigade on its roundabout venture behind the Confederate lines.[24]

The first destination along the protracted and convoluted tour of the southeasternmost hills of the Blue Ridge was the unsuspecting sleepy hamlet of Rutherfordton, North Carolina. Gillem's descent on the town was relatively uneventful, with no surviving reports of malicious canvassing; however, the surrounding rural communities were deeply affected. Taking time to disperse his men into fragments throughout Rutherford County, the steep rolling green countryside was infested by splintered patrols of men as they feinted toward the South Carolina border. The end result of the saturation of the county was that every suitable mount, buggy, valuable, raiment and black male was pilfered or following the command on its venture toward the blue wall. After two days of progressing through Rutherford and Polk Counties, the command arrived at Howard's Gap, a steep incline that had long been the avenue of travel between the upstate of South Carolina and the mountain boroughs of western North Carolina.[25]

As hooves slowly dug into the earth of the steep and winding gap dissecting the mountainous divide of the two Carolinas on the evening of April 22, the men of the Second Brigade were met by volleys loosed by rather reckless home guardsmen and amateur militiamen. This nerve-shattering introduction to the edges of what Carolinians called the "Dark Corner" was most likely spurred by the reassurances of a company of infantry and a battery of artillery that had just that hour abandoned the gap in an effort to bolster the defenses of Asheville. As with most of the desperate late-hour engagements that occurred along the marauders' course, the small band that ambushed the column was greatly outgunned and lacked the steely edge needed to stand its ground—much like the surprised Cherokee braves who were taken from the rear when the pass's namesake ambushed them with the assistance of a young native from a rival tribe over one hundred years earlier.[26]

Although the firing was sporadic, three troopers experienced searing pain induced by the musket balls of the militiamen, leaving one face down in the dark mountain topsoil gasping his dying breath. The recipients of the undisciplined volley, although greatly shaken and startled by the offense, were not to let the affront go unrequited. Wasting no time, junior officers of the lead company sprung into action, ordering their men to dismount and spread into skirmish formation. Advancing under fire through a wind-mangled apple orchard at the base of the steep incline, the advance was swift and effective. Utilizing the advantage of their repeating rifles, the embattled troopers fired while they zigzagged through the blossom-covered orchard.[27]

As the balls from an unseen enemy chipped away at the ancient twisted trunks, the troopers closed the gap between the well-manicured fruit-bearing rows and the more advantageous mountain undergrowth found at the foot of the next ridge. Uncovering a gully at the base of the incline that afforded the skirmishers a vantage point from which to fire upwards on the mountain militia without being subjected to the sporadic discharges of aging muskets, the troopers saturated the laurel thickets that concealed the muzzle flashes of their unseen opponents. Overcome by the unrelenting shower of lead, the mountaineers lost their combative nerve. Turning in flight, the unseen assailants withdrew through the various runs and hollows without a trace, leaving no clues as to their whereabouts or the damage inflicted at the hands of troopers.[28]

With Howard's Gap secured, the command advanced over the crest of the blue wall and made rapid time along the Asheville Highway. It was along this heavily used road that the riders, under command of Major Slater of the Eleventh Kentucky, overtook the battery and infantry that had abandoned the militiamen at Howard's Gap. During the early morning hours of April 23, the Confederate detachment was resting its hoof-sore mounts, having placed much stress on them during its aborted trip from Asheville to Greenville, South Carolina. Having only made it as far as Howard's Gap before they reversed course, the men rested in the cold air of the early spring night waiting for first light to continue their return trip to Asheville.[29]

It was at this point that the troopers, exhausted by an all-night ride bound for Hendersonville, rained down upon the bivouac. The muddled look on the wide, yet still focusing, eyes of the Confederate soldiers was the product of a terror-fraught awakening that can only result when men are reckless enough to bed down in hostile territory without the foresight to post sentries around the camp. Before the majority of the slumbering infantrymen could rouse to answer the screams of their awakened brethren, the troopers were already riding through the midst of them. Without even a shot fired at their blurry adversary, the stunned Confederate soldiers surrendered their precious limbered pieces instead of engaging in a half-delirious Thermopylae.[30]

Adding to their long line of prisoners and camp followers, as well as bringing four prized sets of artillery in tow, Gillem continued his expedition. Advancing through the well-grazed plateaus, farm-dotted mountains and epically steep gorge of the valley, the troopers were in awe of the beauty that was Henderson County. Knowing full well that their adventure through the serene mountains was not a joy ride, the brigade continued along its path with mixed emotions. As one veteran remembered, there was a remorseful sense of disrespect to spoil such an awe-inspiring scene with violence; however, the violation was not without its perks, as virgin plunder awaited in the unsuspecting town of Hendersonville.

In the same vein of entrances witnessed at hamlets such as Boone and Morganton, the raiders burst into Hendersonville generating a ruckus that rivaled any Independence Day celebration experienced by the population in their preceding decades. While the ravishing of Hendersonville was nowhere near the magnitude of that experienced by the residents of other western North Carolina towns, the morning was not without its notable instances. No sooner had the sun climbed a quarter of the way through the sky than one of the last major arms caches found in the practically nonexistent Confederacy fell into the hands of Gillem's men. Riding at the head of the column, the men of the Eleventh Kentucky reported that they had confiscated three hundred stands of arms and accoutrements that were residing in the government storehouses in town, thus drawing the teeth from further resistance in the mountains.[31]

With the men under his immediate command exhausted beyond all means by their protracted trek and confident in the delaying action that was being undertaken by Miller's men in the Third Brigade, Gillem elected to stay the night in Hendersonville. Blind to whether the Confederates in Asheville were still hypnotized by the ruse or had reposition themselves in an effort to intercept the flanking maneuver, the division commander threw a handful of scouts in the direction of his primary target. After receiving encouraging news of the military situation farther down the highway, the general kept his command at ease until shortly after noon on the twenty-third in an effort to afford his men a much-needed opportunity to rest their eyes. Before the Second Brigade departed scenic Hendersonville, Gillem sent a courier toward Lincolnton to instruct Palmer to relocate his headquarters westward to Rutherfordton in preparation of patrolling the southernmost mountain passes of North Carolina.[32]

Unbeknownst to Gillem, on the same day that he entered Hendersonville, the gargantuan obstruction at Swannanoa Gap was lessened. The Legion Infantry under Robert Love was ordered to vacate the works and move with all haste in the direction of Waynesville in an effort to shore up the final vestiges of Confederate influence in the mountains. While the decision to remove one of the last regiments of willful combatants from the defenses of Asheville may have appeared misguided on the surface, the survival of this small band ensured that the Confederacy would be able to continue its resistance in western North Carolina well into the month of May. Coincidently, the very morning that Love's men began their westerly trek toward Waynesville, Gillem's Second Brigade departed Hendersonville for Asheville.[33]

Prior to Gillem's arrival in Asheville, a peace council between General William T. Sherman and General Joseph E. Johnston had convened at the Bennett farmhouse on the outskirts of Durham Station, North Carolina. The summit was very cordial between the two officers, who elected to meet behind closed doors in the inner recesses of the unimposing whitewashed

The Bennett farmhouse as it appeared in a postwar placard. *Courtesy of the Library of Congress.*

home—a stark contrast to the rabblerousing disagreements that were being waged on the exterior of the home by the two armies' subordinate senior officers, which in one instance nearly inaugurated a general row between Confederate chief of cavalry Wade Hampton and the always imposing Union cavalry commander Judson Kilpatrick. The end result of the extended meeting was that both sides were to instantly end any hostilities and observe the status quo of their frontlines in anticipation of word from both shaken governments as to the validity of their negotiated efforts. Unlike the simple terms offered to Lee at the hands of Grant, the peace signed at the Bennett Farm was a negotiated contract between two weary combatants and not a general surrender, thus opening the door to confusion throughout the remaining active theaters of war.[34]

While the Federal troopers were aware of the developments farther east, news of the armistice reached Confederate lines first. It was Martin, the sole Confederate general officer fielding a functional army in the mountains of western North Carolina, who first received the heartbreakingly fortunate news. Having received orders from Johnston to stand down on the night of April 22, Martin quickly moved to place all of his ducks in a row for the inevitable capitulation of Asheville. Since Love's men had already broken camp and were underway, the general disavowed Johnston's directive to stand down and allowed the tiny regiment to continue its course under strict orders to avoid hostilities. No sooner had Love's men departed from eyesight than a local man frantically rode into town bearing news of the large force that had rapidly eaten up the mile markers of the Asheville Highway to occupy nearby Hendersonville.[35]

Knowing that this unseen flanking maneuver by a mysterious Federal commander had made his formidable position at Swannanoa Gap untenable, even without a cessation in hostilities, Martin dispatched Colonel John B. Palmer down the Asheville Highway under escort to personally inform General Gillem of the late-hour developments of the morning of the twenty-third. In the meantime, a staff officer, whose identity is lost to history, rode down the gap to notify Miller's Third Brigade of the agreement between the two rival theater commanders. Instructed to ride hard for the Federal column, the envoys made excellent time, covering all the distance possible by four-legged animals between the city limits of Asheville and the advance guard of the Federal raiders.[36]

It was a Sunday, a full month to the day since most of the men had departed from Morristown, Tennessee. Colonel Palmer of the crumbling army approached the advance guard of Union troopers only a handful of miles from Asheville. It was along that steeply winding dirt byway that the sight of an unarmed rider adorned with the gold-collar stars of a Confederate colonel, clutching a torn white rag at the end of a hardwood limb with a trembling left hand, became the personification of a nightly fantasy that many of the raiders had waited in excess of three years to witness.[37]

Relegating the duty of informing the opposing side of the cessation of hostilities, Palmer edged Lieutenant Davidson from his staff forward to meet face to face with the Federal pickets, who at this juncture were found resting only slightly more than six miles south of the city limits of Asheville. Knowing that contact would most likely be made along the Asheville Highway, Palmer dispatched the lieutenant in that direction while he attempted to ride down Hickory Nut Gap Road in an effort to meet with any rogue elements that might have severed from the command and reach Asheville uninformed of the developments. Dispatches from the Confederate army show that both men reached the advance elements of the Second Brigade simultaneously. The end result of these efforts at contact was that Generals Gillem and Martin would meet at a predetermined spot on the Asheville Highway the morning of April 24.[38]

A few minutes before eleven o'clock on the designated morning of the meeting, Gillem sipped coffee in nervous anticipation of the arrival of an envoy from Martin's Brigade. As calls for the general's location echoed through the bivouac, the old loyalist arose and began to dust himself off in preparation for meeting face to face with what would surely be his prized accomplishment: the surrender of a small Confederate army. However, the alarm was not the heralding of long-awaited political laurels; instead, it was a dispatch rider from the Army of the Tennessee who had arrived with a signed document from none other than General Sherman.

The message detailed a very elaborate and inconvenient order for the general, as all of Stoneman's remaining force was ordered to once again consolidate at Durham Station with Sherman's command. Knowing that this tactical oversight meant the end to his free reign as commander, and that Durham was at the very least twice as far from his present position as was his home base at Greenville, Tennessee, Gillem disavowed the command and ordered his men to make ready for a peaceful return to the volunteer state. Leaving their roadside bivouac, the brigade advanced slowly down the Asheville Highway until it was approximately four miles from Asheville, where Gillem met in council with General Martin.[39]

The meeting vibrated with nervous energy due to the fact that Martin had spent the majority of his wartime career patrolling the mountain passes of western North Carolina, blocking the path of loyalist raiders like Gillem. Hoping for the best, Martin proposed that Gillem would march through Asheville unopposed and draw rations from the Confederate stores that resided there if he would vacate North Carolina for Unionist Tennessee without unsheathing a saber or pilfering a single chicken. Draped in the fraternity that surrounded the two former West Point classmates, the Union command advanced into Asheville under a flag of truce. That evening, the goodwill fostered by the easygoing peace allowed for Gillem and his staff to dine with Martin at his headquarters.[40]

Substantially more cordial than any officer had expected, the dinner conversation was filled with an air of regret for the actions that both devoted commanders had undertaken during the course of the war. Nearing the end of the evening, General Martin pointed out to Gillem that Union control of the telegraph lines and their free-roving couriers placed his force at an unfair advantage should the truce crumble. To offset the advantage, Martin proposed that Gillem allow forty-eight hours' notice before the resumption of hostilities between the two commands as a further sign of the cordiality that was developing in the atmosphere of brotherhood. Without batting an eyelash, Gillem looked Martin in the eyes and enthusiastically agreed to the proposal.[41]

Following the late dinner and the distribution of provisions from the stocks at Asheville, the command wound through the somber streets of the mountain hub late in the evening of the twenty-fifth, with many of the local population observing the procession from their windows and balconies. Accompanying Alvan Gillem, the Second and Third Brigades departed Asheville, undertaking a direct line of march back to Boone and on to Greenville, Tennessee. On the other hand, the First Brigade, under General William Palmer, was ordered to advance by way of Asheville and occupy Waynesville, paying close attention to the Cherokee capital at Quallahtown and the households that dotted the Little Tennessee River Valley.[42]

It was at that point that the chain of command, already retarded by the vacation of Stoneman, broke down entirely. Gillem, hungry for a hand in the cutthroat postwar politics of Reconstruction Tennessee, rode ahead of his command in preparation of expediting his return to Nashville in order to take up his seat in the state legislature. At that point, the three brigades were separated functionally and only held in unison in name alone. Brown, Miller and Palmer simultaneously moved their brigades toward their predetermined destination; however, no one man was at the helm of the division.[43]

Palmer's men, the majority of whom hailed from above the Mason-Dixon line, were taken aback by what they saw on the roads that wound through Rutherford County. Casting eyes on the magnitude of destruction, one survivor in Palmer's First Brigade succinctly summed up the situation when he later remembered that for the mountaineers in the other two brigades, the war was not a martial conflict between two opposing sides. Instead, the war had always been a vehicle for revenge against the misdeeds that the plantation aristocracy had bestowed on them before the war—and later against the hardships bestowed on their families by the Rebel army in the name of eradicating Unionism in the South. The end result was a command so filled with rage that once Stoneman had departed from the scene, their minds became consumed solely with thoughts of revenge. Discipline had collapsed to a point that by the time the two brigades were traveling through Asheville, they had degenerated into a large mob of pirates who could not properly engage an opposing force, no matter how small or ill equipped.[44]

However, their wrath was not always justly directed toward the proper recipients. The shock of the damage left in the wake of Gillem's advance was overwhelming. One recurring theme that budded in the minds of Palmer's veterans was that the privations imposed on the inhabitants of Rutherford County were enacted against a citizenry that was the antonym to

The sobering difference in wealth throughout Appalachia needs no further testament than this late nineteenth-century photograph of the living conditions indicative of generational poverty. *Courtesy of the Library of Congress.*

the definition of affluence. Most of the dirt farmers who drew the majority of the wrath of the demonical mountain loyalists lived in log huts with cedar shingle roofs, scraping a meager near-starving existence from a few worthless rocky acres of iron-encrusted soil. Naturally, these backwoods yokels were not the idealized embodiment of the plantation gentry that their highlands counterparts were reared to loath.[45]

A sight that transformed the shock of the Union men into disgust was the actions of the local gentry minority. Through generations of shiftless land dealings, the upper crust of Rutherford and Polk Counties had cornered the fine bottomland that rolled through the county, the various creeks that constituted the fresh water supply and the flood-prone shallow rivers that yearly swamped the surrounding depleted furrows with fresh topsoil. Coming to the conclusion that this massive disparity was the result of the generational peonage facilitated by the paternalist system governing lowland Southern culture, contempt fermented toward the fancy brick homes that wound through the hills surrounding the Green River. Encouraged by what they had witnessed, the First Brigade arrived at Rutherfordton shortly after nine o'clock on the morning of April 25, looting the town with a ferocity that was extremely atypical of the normally disciplined body. Embittered troopers even went so far as to yank rings from the fingers of local women at gunpoint.[46]

While most of the countryside was devoid of the grand caches that resided within the ornate Southern plantation homes, there were a few notable examples where the troopers burst into the lap of luxury. The stately Green River Plantation was an obvious target of the troopers' wrath. Having somehow escaped the sticky fingers of the ravenous wolves of the First's two sister brigades, the plantation was not as fortunate when the First passed through Polk County. On the afternoon of April 25, the family who dwelled within was visited for only the second time in the war.[47]

Having long feared visitation from lecherous raiders, a slave blacksmith had installed deep-set iron bolts in the doors of the home following the early war death of the plantation heir-apparent. While a small band of loyalists had plucked the chickens from the property and had their run of the storehouse two autumns earlier, the plantation was relatively virgin property for a fragment of the First Brigade when it ventured up the long dirt driveway. After barging into the home and taking their pick of the few valuables that the family's slaves had not buried over the two previous years, the troopers brought their horses inside to stable them in the first-story drawing room. While some have suspected that the stabling of mounts

In astounding contrast to the hovels that littered the landscape, the stately Green River Plantation was a natural beacon for those looking to line their saddlebags by extracurricular sightseeing. *Courtesy of the Library of Congress.*

inside the main house was intended as an insult toward the family, others have suspected that the small patrol was being pursued by a larger force of local home guard and believed it would be easier to avoid detection by resting the horses inside the large home. The following morning, the handful of intruders departed without incident and returned to the main column, leaving only scores of deep hoof prints in the wood floor of the plantation house as a reminder of their visit.[48]

Upon receiving the third change of assignments in as many days, Palmer's men readjusted their course from Rutherfordton and made for the most direct route to the Little Tennessee River. At the same time that the First Brigade was beginning to ride toward Jackson County, Brown and Miller reversed course, most likely under orders from Stoneman, who was instructed by Sherman to recommence his activities in light of a floundering truce with the Confederates. Without any recorded or preserved order, the pair fell back on an undefended Asheville with their two brigades. Less than a day following the cordial exodus of the troopers, the unsuspecting city of Asheville was to finally receive the long-anticipated sacking that it had feared since the inauguration of war.[49]

Trouble began for the mountain hub on the afternoon of April 24, when Stoneman received a wire from General George H. Thomas informing him that the truce between Sherman and Johnston had been overturned by President Andrew Johnson. The new president, a former illiterate Union democrat from East Tennessee—like many of his constituents—wished to see the cotton aristocracy crushed once and for all. Believing that it was pertinent for Sherman to press his military advantage and extort from Johnston the same conditional capitulation that had been imposed on Lee by Grant, the president urged Sherman forward against the Rebel lines. Following news of this unfortunate turn of events, Stoneman ordered his command to move in unison with Sherman.[50]

The logical course of action for the three brigades was to reverse course, retracing their steps back to Salisbury and finally completing the insubordinately ignored linkup with Sherman near Durham Station. While the reversal in course by the division was to be expected considering the nature of the order, what remains a mystery are the motivations for the actions taken by the Second and Third Brigades upon their arrival at Asheville. Reneging

Although born in North Carolina, the beset new president Andrew Johnson intimately understood the Unionist goals of East Tennessee as their political benefactor. *Courtesy of the Library of Congress.*

While not exactly a benefactor, Virginia native and western theater hero George H. Thomas took exorbitant steps to keep his friend George Stoneman in the saddle. *Courtesy of the Library of Congress.*

Perceived as cautious to a fault by his contemporaries and decidedly against the continuation of the desperate struggle, Joseph E. Johnston in no way held the confidence of the commander-in-chief. Although at constant odds with his civilian superior, it was the efforts of the reserved general that salvaged the Confederate war effort following the surrender at Appomattox. *Courtesy of the Library of Congress.*

the agreed upon grace period of forty-eight hours before the continuation of hostilities, the troopers under Brown and Miller descended on Asheville like a swarm of ravenous locusts driven by an appetite that could only be abated through indiscriminate destruction.

Shortly after dark on April 26, the sister brigades rode into Asheville, much to the unsuspecting surprise of the few pickets that were posted around the town. After cunningly passing into the interior lines of the few remaining Confederate infantry in Asheville, a general row exploded between the devious troopers and the bewildered defenders. Following the first salvos of the troopers, the overwhelmed, insufficiently armed and surrounded infantrymen shucked their weapons and lifted their arms into the moonlight. The end results of the sudden wrangling of the rebellious infantry were thirty officers and forty enlisted men taken into custody.[51]

Knowing that the command was most likely faced with a protracted overland ride into the central counties of the state, a long procession of prisoners was an impediment that the pair of brigade commanders could not afford. Thinking of the benefits of greater mobility, the enlisted men were paroled on site. The disbelieving captives nervously signed their parole sheets, while communally sharing with their capitulated brethren the unspoken understanding that any contract made with these backstabbing scoundrels was less than reassuring. Meanwhile, steps were taken to transport the thirty officers under guard to Knoxville in preparation of sending the unfortunate souls north.[52]

With the outermost defenders of the city under thumb, the raiders flooded into Asheville at lightning speed, combing the streets for targets of opportunity. In an obvious affront to the brotherhood afforded the officers, Confederate General Martin was arrested at his home on the outskirts of Asheville and sent before Brown for interrogation. After a tense hour of conversation—a stark contrast to the pleasant banter that the two had engaged in just the previous evening—Martin divulged all the information that the Michigander demanded. Most likely forced to outline critical intelligence pertaining to the remaining Confederate forces in the region, Martin was dismissed without a parole offer and instructed to return to his home to await further orders.[53]

Arriving at his home, Martin was welcomed by an unsuspected sight. Brown had been studious enough to dispatch a guard detail in the general's absence to ensure the well-being of his family and hearth. Dismounting and scouring his boots at the base of the veranda, the general exchanged a few seconds of cordialness with the troopers who had dutifully watched over his family. However, as he entered his home, the general was greeted with a shockingly unexpected sight.[54]

There he found his wife and daughters leading several members of the squad by candlelight through the house. As the shadows danced on the wall, the unruly troopers extracted whatever objects they fancied on their grand tour of the home—a veritable shopping spree at the general's expense. Upon Martin's protest of the spectacle, the junior officer abided the irate Confederate and ordered his plunderers to abandon their venture, yet nothing was said concerning the true ownership of the newfound possessions that lined the troopers' pockets. The remainder of the night was uneasy, as the post remained to protect the family whom they had just looted.[55]

The demonical violence displayed toward the civilians of Asheville at the hands of the troopers launched a general transformation in the nature of the raid. Increasingly, the need to secure last-minute postwar financial acumen took priority over the need to fulfill their martial duty, and the end result was a progressively more sinister approach toward civilians. In every direction, bewildered citizens were taken aback by representatives of the Federal government run amok. Untold thousands of dollars in valuables were pried from the clutches of their owners, and as the treasures dwindled in number, so increased the ferocity of the troopers' search for the remains.

At the summer home of Judge Bailey, the troopers entered without announcement through a glassed-in porch, shattering the glass with their rifle butts as they scaled its height. As the troopers poured into the family room—which was inhabited by Bailey, his son who was a paroled Confederate officer from the Army of Northern Virginia, his daughters and his wife—the aging judge instinctively lifted a revolver from a nearby table. Leveling the revolver and threatening to dispatch the first trooper who advanced on his family, the judge rose to his feet while motioning his family to the opposite end of the room. The decision proved to be unwise, as the solitary revolver was met by the cold muzzles of a half dozen Spencer repeating rifles.[56]

Outgunned by approximately twenty calibers and six times over, the judge was saved by the quick thinking of his son, who divulged his identity in an effort to prevent the diffusion of his father's blood. Lowering his pistol after a sense of hopelessness overcame the adrenaline rush produced by the soldiers' entrance, Bailey conceded to the troopers. As the un-cocked revolver plummeted to the floor, the troopers stormed into the room. Scattering throughout the chamber with unspoken orders, a few of the intruders wrangled the twenty-something officer into submission, while one slighted raider rattled the judge's brain with a rifle butt stroke to his forehead.[57]

Vacating the premises with the unconscious judge's son in custody, the trooper at whom the judge had directly leveled his pistol could not let the offense go unanswered. After a few moments of frantic pacing and filling the night air with some of the most malicious cursing ever emoted, the trooper turned to once again climb the steps of the porch. Drawing the hammer of his carbine to the firing position, the trooper unleashed a solitary round from the hip, aimed at the head of the semiconscious judge. Fortunately for the judge, rage, carelessness or inebriation inhibited the trooper's marksmanship, leaving the bullet harmlessly lodged in the door of the home just a few meager feet from the spot where it was discharged.[58]

Aside from the affront placed on the family by the heavy hands of the troopers, the home was thoroughly looted. Naturally, all silver and gold trinkets were taken from the home during the original visitation. Following the procurement of the treasure-trove that was tucked away in the judge's home, the family was afforded no respite, as a revolving door of troopers flowed through the house in search of sustenance and an opportunity to pick the bones of the family's rapidly depleting fortune. Afterward, the thieves elected to remain on the site and slumbered in the outbuildings of the property.[59]

Rising to his feet following a skull-jarring nap, the judge walked to Asheville and visited the domicile inhabited by an unmentioned Federal colonel. Infuriated by news of the outrage, which was substantiated by the judge's blood-crusted forehead, the colonel ordered a detail to assist the muddled man home and to chase away interlopers. The scene, which was queerly repeated by both sides in the conflict, pitted orderly soldiers against criminals masquerading in government-issued uniforms. With the task accomplished, the detail remained until sunup, at which point the obedient troopers left to seek out breakfast at some unspoiled venue in the sacked town.[60]

No sooner had the guards departed than a third cluster of raiders arrived at the home to ransack the pantries and smokehouses. The end result was that every ounce of cured meat was lifted from its rack and tucked inside the burlap sacks that the men had procured from the property. Under protest from the judge's wife, a solitary pork shoulder was cast at her feet. As the romantic tradition of the cotton aristocracy holds, the appeal was not made in an effort to feed the dwellers of the main house; instead, the plea was made on behalf of the depleted stomachs of the poor black servants who manned the opulent vacation home.[61]

Early the following morning, Judge Bailey and his daughter walked to Asheville with the intention of visiting with their incarcerated family member. The pandemonium, which awaited them with open arms, was unlike anything that they expected from the sleepy mountain town. The first in a long line of offenses experienced by the pair came when the black soldiers who had attached themselves to Miller's command began to heckle the judge, asking the still sore legalist how he liked their appearance in the blue uniform. This offense, however slight, was one from which the family never recovered, leading to a long-standing grudge against the Union and the black race.[62]

Aside from the transgression delivered by the emancipated warriors, the most shocking development for the duo was the sight of the Union banner being suspended from the second-story terrace of the Old Eagle Hotel. It was noted by the judge's daughter that the women of town went out of their way to bypass the hotel via a parallel street. The silent protest was craftily executed so as not to give the raiders the satisfaction of seeing them obediently walk under the auspices of the grand old flag.[63]

Continuing their journey, the pair found that the Central Bank of Asheville was being utilized as an impromptu prison and was stuffed to capacity with a congregation of Confederate officers. The senior captive in the room was none other than Colonel Robert Love, who had been intercepted on the road that connected Waynesboro to Asheville. After visiting with their beloved prisoner, who was in far better shape than the venturing pair expected, the duo vacated the bank only to meet a familiar chattel uncle who confronted them with hat in hand and eyes affixed at the dirt beneath his feet.[64]

The apologetic Negro outlined the core reason for the ills that had befallen the unsuspecting home that previous evening. He explained that the troopers had cornered him on an Asheville street and leveled a pistol in his face, demanding that the old man lead them to the judge's house so they might take his watch. Attempting to con his way out of the deadly conundrum, the old man contritely explained that the judge was no longer in possession of such an accessory due to his commitment to the war effort. Not falling for the ruse, or with their minds already made up to ransack the judge's home, the offending trooper drew back the hammer and threatened to alleviate the old slave of the weight of his head unless he cooperated. With the tepidly damp sensation of free-flowing urine down the legs of his trousers being the least of his problems, the old man regrettably obliged.[65]

Although the damage had been done by the time the command departed late on the morning of April 27, the region still suffered from the occupation of rogue troopers. Fortunately for the prisoners of Asheville, a consolation development had broken in their favor as electric pulses raced along the telegraph wires that connected Knoxville and Rutherfordton. General

William J. Palmer of the First Brigade was appointed by Stoneman as Gillem's heir to command the division. On the same day that the troopers of the Second and Third Brigades descended on the most populous town in western North Carolina, the favorable shift in command was made.[66]

Having been informed of the havoc inflicted by the other two brigades as he headed for the Little Tennessee River about mid-afternoon on the twenty-seventh, Palmer instantly exercised the authority bestowed upon him. His first action as division commander was to seek out an undisturbed line and telegraph both Brown and Miller that their deplorable actions were to cease immediately. Furthermore, the new commander ordered all prisoners released to their homes, their extorted paroles disavowed and the issuance of a formal apology to the citizens of Asheville and the former officers of the Confederate army. Naturally, the foundation for this decision was grounded in the fact that the leaders of the two brigades had violated a separate truce from the disavowed agreement negotiated between Sherman and Johnston.[67]

As Palmer departed Rutherfordton on the afternoon of the twenty-sixth and the other brigades of the division victoriously vacated Asheville past the meridian on the twenty-seventh, a peculiar development unfolded that would greatly influence the lives of the troopers for the next couple of weeks. Believing that their role in the war was complete, and that their bodies had survived the fratricide intact, the troopers were soon to become the recipients of shatteringly unexpected news. As sparks raced down the telegraph wire, it was soon learned that the command was to engage in the pursuit of a fugitive that would take them from the mountains of western North Carolina, through the unspoiled pastures of the Palmetto State and on to the university greens of Georgia. The pursuit of the renegade Confederate president Jefferson Davis would not only become a laurel-laden quest but also an excellent opportunity to take advantage of the confusion and disorder of the closing weeks of the war, giving license to the sticky palms of the Second and Third Brigades to come away from the conflict with more than the promise of a meager pension that was to be delivered decades in the future.

2
"We Have Now Entered Upon a New Phase of the Struggle"

The crags of this country truly are remarkable." The tart taste and cleansing aroma of murky ambrosia penetrated his senses to combine with the warm radiation of a slowly cooling tin cup. Forming a perfectly serene ambiance as his pulsating hand lifted the steaming chalice to his chapped lips in preparation for yet another sip of coffee, the reflective partaker mused, "I doubt such providence-inspired views will ever again befall my eyes."

As the muted rumble generated by the lengthy cascade of water from the falls flowing from the opposite ridge further titillated his senses, the freshly brevetted general of volunteers lightheartedly walked away from the campfire in search of a new position from which he could further enjoy the view that their bivouac opposite Hickory Mountain afforded. Content with the progress that his weary men had made and certain that the conflict would be over before week's end, a long overdue smirk crossed the benevolent face. Looking out over the sapphire haze that wove through the early mountain morning, the captain of the raid lost himself in contemplation as the frosty sensation of highland spring mist pelted his face. "The push up the Hickory Nut Gap last evening was worth it. This may very well be the most pleasant awakening of the war."[68]

Sliding his weight atop a wind-swept rock until his feet disappeared into oblivion over its edge, the magnitude of affinity that his men held for him was evident in the reactions of a cluster of privates leisurely conversing at its foot. Shuffling for the right grove in which to rest his haunches, the general officer momentarily locked eyes with his subordinates. The trio beneath acknowledged his presence with nothing more than a nod common to those exchanged between old friends. Indeed, the Fifteenth Pennsylvania Cavalry Regiment truly had evolved into a close-knit family after three years of hellish suffering.

The meditative serenity induced by blue mist shrouding the early morning skyline came to an untimely end as William's name came echoing from some unknown point along the rock-encrusted side of Hickory Mountain. Taken aback by the unexpected anomaly, he could not help but wonder if the architects of such a view were themselves calling out to him. Reality, however, ruined any foray into the comforts of his imagination. The momentarily perplexed lounger felt a flood of private embarrassment overcome him, feeling shame for suspecting that anything other than the simple reverberation of an echo was the culprit. Shaking off his late-life burst of childish wonder, the general averted his eyes from the natural spectacle only to be greeted by the sight of a staff officer clumsily skipping down the decline of the mountain bald.

"William." The faux familiarity emerged with an unnatural shakiness from the lieutenant's throat, as his sense of etiquette still wrestled with the growing cordiality that had taken root in the unwinding volunteer regiment. "A courier has just arrived with this dispatch." Understanding that any news that was prefaced with a qualifier spelled trouble, the junior officer remorsefully sighed. "The rider was a sergeant and said that the message is urgent." As the general instantly drew back from the edge of the rock and rose to his feet, the surprise that the messenger held such an uncommon rank for an errand boy drowned out the natural beauty that had hypnotized him just a few seconds earlier.

"Urgent you say?" he asked, understanding that the gravity borne in the introduction had instantly doomed any hope he held of experiencing the cloud-like comfort of a dry bed and the refreshing steam of a hot bath. He resigned himself to the unfortunate news of the still unseen order: "Have the bugler sound first call for an officers' meeting."

Reaching into his left pocket and extracting a weathered walnut-handled jackknife marred with the dull sheen of permanent fingerprints from years of repetitive use, the frustrated officer tore through the twine that bound the envelope with its unsheathed blade. Knowing full well in the deep recesses of his bowels that the war still held a few surprises in store, the general's heart was conspicuously void of the sinking sensation that would have been expected of a man in possession of a weaker constitution as he perused the tattered, sun-bleached dispatch that was penned by the raid's father in

Tennessee. Dissecting the drop-ink product of an unsung scribe's tedious effort with increasingly stoic eyes, the bloodshot saucers expanded as they jerked from left to right. The news, while detailing a long-dreaded extension to the taxing canvassing that his boys had regrettably become accustomed to, held a rather unsuspecting twist that no soothsayer without the luxury of hindsight could have predicted.

"Thirteen million in gold? Christ, I thought this fiasco would have been settled with the fall of Richmond, the dissolution of Lee's army or along any of those goddamned miles of track that we twisted!" The loathing rise of disbelief soared from his loins and swelled the pulsating veins in his temples. "Why did Sheridan fail to settle this?" Rereading the dispatch in an effort to absorb the momentous task and all of the peculiar nuances that this extraordinary directive held, Palmer reflected, "This war will never end." Turning against the awe-inspiring beauty that only a moment before had delighted his senses, he declared, "I will never leave this Godforsaken region; my entire life will be spent bringing this rebellion to a close." Exerting the effort of a third reading, an unwanted burden emerged from the intricate webbing of letters.[69]

"Obedience only to Stanton, disavow Sherman, ignore Thomas, sever myself from Stoneman, impunity from any directive given by a senior officer in the field and disavow the concept of superior rank as a whole." His free hand removed his hat and simultaneously stroked the tusk of hair that it concealed as the officer processed the ambiguous nature of this unprecedented order. Understanding that his day-old commission as the commander of a light cavalry division had been exponentially expanded, Palmer drew another sip from his lukewarm coffee. Brooding as his mind walked through the possibility of a campaign without a stationary objective, he thought, "I hope this affair is settled before summer. I cannot stomach another humid summer in Georgia." It was with this thought that a reality all too foreign to the military came crashing down on the thinker: his commission was devoid of any subordinate measure, and he was as close to a liberated commander as a mounted officer could be.[70]

In a war that experienced unprecedented civilian meddling in the day-to-day affairs of the military, the orders thrust into Palmer's free hand as his command rested on a ridge near Hickory Mountain on the morning of April 27 were some of the most fervent examples of the abuse of authority by the executive branch that can be found in the annals of the war. The contents of the tattered envelope were many days in the making. With its origins in the late evening evacuation of Richmond on April 2 and accelerating

Once acknowledged by Lincoln as the rock on which the surf of hostilities broke as it assaulted the beach, Edwin McMasters Stanton was the bulwark of the administration. After the death of his consummate understudy and sometimes benefactor, Stanton took up a personal vendetta against the insolent Confederate hierarchy that remained in the field. *Courtesy of the Library of Congress.*

with the April 14 assassination of the renegade president's counterpart while he jovially unraveled his years of stress as a troupe performed their lines from the beginning of the third act of *Our American Cousin* at Ford's Theater, the assignment reeked of intrigue and fanatical pettiness. After the contemplative canyons of the weary Great Emancipator's face became devoid of tone and still to emotion forever, his successor was overwhelmed by the politics of the ghostly administration, the war and the Goliath that was known as Secretary of War Edwin Stanton. With the untimely lam of the fugitive Confederate president, the megalomaniacal mindset taken by Stanton and tales of a renegade fortune rocketing through every rumor mill found in the taverns of the Union armies, the exhausted men and mounts of Palmer's division were to become pawns in an unnecessary checkmate on secession.[71]

The orders that Palmer cast his eyes upon that morning redefined the mission of his division and the legacy of the raid. The Delawarean was given complete anonymity from the desires of his superior theater commanders, no matter on what side of the Appalachian Mountains his men may have found themselves during their new adventure. Furthermore, he was instructed to pursue the man mislabeled as the villain of the war to the ends of the earth.

Owing allegiance only to Secretary of War Edwin Stanton, aided by a $100,000 head bounty and cut loose from the hindrance of the peacefully conflicting orders of democratic generals such as William T. Sherman and George H. Thomas, the orphans of Stoneman's grand design were to travel to points southwest of their Appalachian positions. Cresting the Blue Ridge once again to follow the edge of the Cherokee Foothills of South Carolina and pick up on the lingering scent of one of the last men who still believed in the vitality of the Confederacy, the exhausted men of the three brigades were to ride harder than ever before. While the $100,000 reward for Jefferson Davis made a handsome prize in and of itself, the true target of the increasingly unruly troopers' ambition were the massive wagonloads of treasure rumored to be strategically placed under the renegade president's derriere on his odyssey toward the Mississippi River and the Confederate holdings beyond.[72]

While the rumors of Rebel treasure have been a novelty of conversation for generations, what is known to history is that the Confederate treasury was lovingly packaged and placed on train cars on the night of April 2 while the Gibraltar of Petersburg crumbled. However, the extent of that treasure has been hotly debated since the night that Rebel bankers drove the final nail of the last crate home. Stanton, now the closest thing that the country had to an executive since the tragic death of Rosewatery Lincoln, estimated the Confederate horde in the stratosphere of $13 million in gold. This impressive haul left most soldiers salivating; however, many were skeptical.[73]

Cooler heads, such as George H. Thomas, advised Stoneman that the bullion was perhaps as low in number as $2 million. Regardless of the monetary value of the wayward cache, the mission remained unaffected. Palmer's men, and their two sister brigades under Brown and Miller, were to strike out immediately, without the benefit of division-wide consolidation, and to reverse their course for the Palmetto State. Much to the everlasting regret of the population of the upstate of South Carolina, as the splintered division entered the region in a piecemeal fashion, the command structure became practically nonexistent for large sections of the column.[74]

Loosing curriers in the direction of Asheville and Flat Rock, Palmer brought his column about-face and once again followed the Hickory Nut Gap, this time bound for the last vestige of commerce that his eyes had befallen: Rutherfordton. The visitation upon the afflicted town was fleeting, as Palmer's men only requisitioned corn and a few suitable mounts before resuming their journey without respite. Before departing, however, Palmer instructed the local printing press commandeered in an effort to print up a suitable amount of wanted posters that were to be placed sporadically along their line of march. With the commission fulfilled, and the large classical type advertising the exorbitant reward for the members of the fugitive party nailed to every point of interest along their path, the brigade departed the rattled hamlet for the border that dissected the Carolinas. It was April 29, and the column was bound for what was then known as Yorkville, South Carolina—a crossroads that slumbered on the eastern corner of the Piedmont.[75]

The late April descent of the main body into South Carolina was not the first time the raiders had trampled the soil of the Palmetto State. A week earlier, while the First Brigade was active around Lincolnton, elements of the command had forded the Catawba River in order to exploit the bounty of a series of boroughs originally known as the Waxhaws. The once impoverished backwoods communities, which had blossomed into prosperity with the explosion of the uplands cotton economy, were the ancestral homes to many of the antebellum giants of United States politics—most notably John C. Calhoun.[76]

Understanding that any man-made structure spanning a swift-moving river such as the Catawba was of great benefit to the enemy, it was mutually agreed upon by Stoneman and his subordinates that even though the conflict was subsiding, structures that immediately benefited Davis were to be rendered useless. Having neutralized Basil Duke's cavalry in the area, the men of the First Brigade turned their attention to infrastructure. On April 19, men belonging to the Twelfth Ohio and the Fifteenth Pennsylvania sought to deprive the South of its grip on the Catawba River Bridge that towered over Nations Ford. Although the random elements of Duke's command were easily persuaded to abandon their delaying action, as realization that the final moments of the conflict were ticking by, the local home guard that protected the high-valued wooden structure had other opinions as to the validity of the Confederate cause—no doubt derived from their late-hour naivety toward the true nature of the war.[77]

Falling under the leadership of an unremembered local officer, the home guard had spent the past week preparing for their long-awaited stand. Blocking the road that led to numerous untouched communities, the south bank of the river was heavily fortified just beyond the bridge. The fortification was impressive for such a hectic undertaking. Encompassing nearly twenty yards of high walls that covered the front and flanks, the centerpiece was an entrenched artillery piece of unspecified dimension.[78]

The image of the fight that followed is murky due to a major pitfall of local history: a lack of documentation. Aside from an apathetically scribbled dispatch from the battalion's commander and the smoldering ruins of a bridge, neither combatant left any solid documentation. Arriving within sight of their target about mid-morning, the members of the First Brigade who had accompanied Major Erastus C. Moderwell to the bridge were in no mood to mince words with the ignorantly audacious defenders. Dismounting and drawing into line of battle, the battalion of about four hundred strong surveyed the possible avenues of assault. Instantly, a windfall of luck caught their attention; the amateur soldiers had not had the foresight to remove the boards from the floor of the bride. With the position foolishly left open to a full-on charge, their task appeared to be exponentially easier than the saddle-weary troopers had anticipated.[79]

In short order, two skirmish lines were formed on the flanks of the bridge, and a harassing fire was let loose upon the opposing bank. Peppering a well-constructed wall of red clay, this nonlethal barrage screamed across the river in an effort to attract the attention of the only tool in the home guard's possession that concerned the raiders: the artillery piece zeroed-in on the center of the bridge. As the defenders' Enfield rifles responded sporadically, the cannon was repositioned to drive off the harassing skirmish line. A few moments later, the swift waters of the Catawba rippled with the reverberation of an inaugural salvo, unleashing a round that landed short of the troopers and inflicted no carnage whatsoever. Advancing while the cannoneers reloaded their behemoth, the battalion of troopers closed in on the mouth of the bridge.[80]

The advance was only slightly pressured by the intermittent fire of the militia. With a well-disciplined barrage cast upon their position, the earthwork's inhabitants stayed close to the ground in an effort to keep their skulls intact. Unable to see the gun crew move into firing position from its poor vantage point, the advance was taken off guard by the impact of the second round in the middle of the road, just a few feet from the north end of the bridge. Keeping with its amateur shenanigans, once again, the projectile netted no fruit.[81]

Two times was chance enough for many of the assaulters. Knowing that the cannoneers were readying yet another thunderbolt and that the towering position of the home guard was hard enough to crack against nervous amateurs, much less a body of about forty to eighty determined men, the troopers abandoned their assault. Withdrawing to a safe distance, the rejected riders continued to strafe the Confederate-held south bank. With the rapid snap of brass cartridges filling the sulfur-choked morning breeze, an unexpected sight befell their eyes.[82]

As members of the Fifteenth Pennsylvania resituated to avoid the thundering iron giant's wrath, scouts were dispatched along both flanks in search of an advantageous ford to cross and check their stubborn adversaries. In the midst of a brisk shuffle toward defilade, one or two of the troopers began to motion to their officers in an attempt to direct attention to the bridge. At first, it looked as if the morning's fog was burning off the cool water of the river. That assumption, however, was quickly abandoned as steady plumes of smoke began to rise from numerous points along the bridge's foundation. In a surprising turn of events, the adamant defenders were incinerating the very object of their affection.[83]

Seeing that the plumes had mushroomed into flame-augmented bellows, the home guardsmen began to frantically shuffle about in their earthworks, no doubt making good their escape. Content to sit back and observe the bridge reduce itself from a safe distance, the troopers watched as the cannon crew attempted to spike their gun. The traditional last resort of cannoneers was undoubtedly a halfhearted undertaking, since there was no fire in which to heat a cut nail to a temperature that would allow it to seal the vent effortlessly. Instead, the home guard drove whatever iron object they had at their disposal down the vent, leaving the gun in salvageable condition should Union blacksmiths care to attempt such a task at this late hour in the war.[84]

While the amateur spiking of the tube was to be expected, what happened next was totally foreign to the eyes of the veteran troopers. In an effort to prevent a rout, the rearguard of the fleeing militia continued to exchange martial banter with the skirmishers. Meanwhile, the cannoneers hauled their piece from the rear of the earthworks and repositioned it east of the roadbed. Drawing the attention of almost every trooper who was curious to see how the strange actions of the gun crew would play out, nary a soul directed a lead slug in their direction. Sizing up the slope of the riverbank, the Confederates situated their gun atop a natural cut in the hillside. Digging their heels into the warm April grass, the team built up momentum as it drove the artillery piece toward the river.[85]

Finally, in one last exhaustive shove, the cannon was released to its own self-determination as it neared the steep slope of the riverbank. Slicing deep into the bank with its stock, the cannon left a distinctive furrow as it reached the precipice. Not waiting to watch their beloved friend plummet into the muddy south bank of the Catawba, the cannoneers turned and ran along with the rearguard. Cheering in comical approval as the cannon reached what was thought to be a watery grave—although it was later recovered by the home guardsmen with the use of a logging chain and made serviceable again by a local blacksmith in the closing days of the war—a few of the troopers cautiously advanced down to the north bank.[86]

Inspecting the extent of the blaze that the Confederates had set under their bridge, it was clear that the structure would collapse in due time. Although a generation later, Confederate recollections made note that the raiders had incinerated the bridge by pouring lamp oil on it, this claim can only be substantiated in the exaggerations of elder storytellers with an audience. The damage was total as flames began to dance amongst the floorboards. Satisfied with this fortunate development, the battalion remounted and made a swift return to Lincolnton.[87]

Even though the Fifteenth Pennsylvania was momentarily stationed at Lincolnton in an effort to observe the Catawba River, a handful of its members took license with their patrols and entered the virgin hills of South Carolina in an effort to procure advantageous plunder. At Black Jack Plantation outside Fort Mill, the residence of a local doctor by the surname of Avery, some of the rogue adventurers engaged in their newfound pastime. Leaving the home unmolested, troopers turned their attention to the outbuildings and led away the majority of the doctor's stock, approximately twelve beasts in all. Informed of the raiders' presence in the area and fearing visitation, the family had already sought refuge in a home of modest means inside Fort Mill proper. Concern harbored for the estate was well founded, as one of the family's chattel arrived that afternoon with word that the plantation was visited and the livestock pilfered.[88]

Striking out for Black Jack Plantation with a local able-bodied male, William Killian, Doctor Avery and his follower eventually made it to the property and validated the story his slave had told him. Not content to sit idly by and face near ruin in the upcoming summer months due to the absence of draft animals on the property, the pair rode out in the direction of North Carolina, hoping to recover some of the purloined animals. The sights that confronted them along the road that led toward the Catawba River were unlike any that had previously befallen their eyes.[89]

Having secured ample replacements for their emaciated mounts, the roadbed was littered with subpar equines. They were nearing starvation and struck lame with a plethora of ailments, and Avery remembered that he had never before—and never since—seen such poor examples of horseflesh. As the couple progressed farther down the road, the larger their collection became. The harvest of thin flesh was not to go uninterrupted, as the scavengers haphazardly hoofed into range of the raiders' rearguard.[90]

The path of the raid was littered with emaciated animals, run to the point of exhaustion or injury. *Courtesy of the Library of Congress.*

As shots rang out from the unseen position the ambushers were holding, several of the newly acquired animals were riddled with projectiles. The hollow thuds of lead boring through animal carcasses were augmented with another sound entirely foreign to Avery's ears. Hearing a thump of a different resonance, the doctor turned to see William Killian stumble and fall to the ground, struck through the bowels with a Federal slug. Throwing William on top of a nearby mount, the pair withdrew from the range of the troopers, who elected not to pursue them.[91]

Seeking refuge at the nearby home of Eugene Hutchinson, the doctor and resident manservant moved Killian to a comfortable couch in the first-floor parlor. Attempts by Avery to apply his avocation upon his suffering companion without proper implements were in vain. Although the young man's fate was sealed, Avery took it upon himself to send word to the family about their unknown misfortune in hopes that an impromptu reunion might bring some comfort in the dying man's final moments.

Leaving his fellow traveler with the mistress of the house and her manservant, Avery set out for Fort Mill at once. Riding down the road at a full gallop, the doctor was nearly unseated from his mount by a misdirected round from a Federal straggler. Ordering the doctor to halt with a fresh round securely housed in his Spencer, the embattled messenger had no choice but to oblige the command. Slowly dismounting, the doctor did his best to withhold the flushness that normally deepened the tone of his face when he was enraged—and this stranger's audacity had established a pinnacle of ire that was never surpassed.[92]

Determined not to let his friend die alone, Avery waited for the opportune moment to strike. Sensing a lapse in vigilance that would last long enough to afford a proper inspection of the mount, the aging doctor demonstrated unprecedented bravado for his gentle station in society and lunged for the unsecured carbine. The struggle lasted for only a moment. Completely taken aback by the sudden onslaught, the trooper panicked and struggled over possession of the contested rifle, failing to draw his available revolver and instantly end the competition in his favor.[93]

Instead, the surprise proved to be too much, and the situation deteriorated in a flash. As a result of unsure footing, the trooper's knees buckled, and he collapsed under his own weight. Quickly regaining his bearings, he found himself on his back, staring down the barrel of his own primary weapon. In just two dozen seconds, the bottom rail had found its way to the top, and a bested raider was at the mercy of his former prisoner.

Understanding full well the conundrum in which he presently found himself, the trooper slowly unfastened his holster and discarded his revolver, soon followed by his saber and other implements of destruction. Although the doctor had the upper hand, the arrangement was not to his advantage, as surely his prisoner's rearguard counterparts would notice his absence and come in search of him. The awkward journey back to Fort Mill was full of nervous tension as thoughts of what to do with his captive and the possible repercussions to his family should the troopers find out swam through his head. If he was unable to shuck the prisoner before his arrival and was later found to be in possession of the search party's compatriot, then wrath of untold ferocity could be unleashed on the town. Nearly contented to lead his former antagonist to a nearby grove and execute him, Avery received the gentile smile of fortune in his darkest hour.

Looking off toward the road leading into Fort Mill, the dust that rose from the highway was a sure sign that the doctor was about to meet his demise, shot as a spy by the approaching search party for holding a Federal soldier against his will. As the body of mounted men approached, however, Avery was relieved to observe that the men were not Federal troopers. Instead, the approaching riders belonged to a fraction of Joseph Wheeler's column that was shadowing the advance of Stoneman. More than happy to surrender his captive to the troopers, whose fate was never told, Avery departed the scene to fulfill his somber task of delivering the unfortunate news to the Killian family.[94]

Although the arrival of Wheeler's men brought momentary relief to Avery, as with similar experiences of Confederate civilians allayed by the mute tones of their uniforms, the arrival of the western cavalry troopers was not without its pitfalls. Naturally, by this late hour in the war, April 19, discipline had so eroded in both armies that civilians had to be equally wary of those riding under both banners. Even before this tragic day witnessed first light, bands of outliers and renegades had begun to swell their ranks with soldiers who had taken to self-preservation and advancement.

The first step toward this transformation, widely experienced throughout both armies like an addictive epidemic, was advantageous pilfering—and virgin territory throughout the upstate was ripe for deflowering. As the flora of April began to retreat for the year, hundreds had already succumbed to the addiction and joined renegade bands. Should the war have limped into the fall of 1865, there was a distinct possibility that the mounted elements of both sides would have reverted to a primal state so ferocious that they would have been more of a liability to their commanders than an attribute.

Fully aware that Federal raiders were in the area, Nee Mattie Steele had taken exorbitant steps to protect her family's final possessions from the invaders' greedy paws. Understanding that time was of the essence, the male members of her family had gathered the majority of the livestock, surplus provisions and human property that remained on the homestead. Abandoning the fairer sex, the male stalwarts fled the path of the raiders by heading off toward the Blue Ridge in search of refuge.[95]

Left alone to guard the homestead, Mrs. Steele spent the days surrounding the nineteenth gathering intrinsic possessions. Among her few remaining treasures not bartered away over the previous three years were a small jewelry box and three pocket watches left her by her father. Determined that the small nest egg was not to leave her possession, a stroke of genius crossed her mind. Removing her underwear, she fashioned a bindle from a bedsheet and attached it to the garment's undercarriage, all in an effort to comfortably merge her wealth and virtue into one.[96]

To cover the conspicuous bulge, Steele fastened three of her prized dresses to her narrow frame. The excess not only served as an effective veil for the prize but also kept the valuable raiment out of the raiders' hands. For three days, she nervously paced around the homestead awaiting the arrival of Federal troopers. Her fears were unwarranted, as the men of Stoneman's column never arrived. However, riders belonging to Wheeler's command did.[97]

Hearing the impact of hooves as they echoed through her open windows, she knew that the fateful moment had arrived. Stricken with foolhardy inspiration, she sprang to her feet at the very last moment. For reasons that remained a mystery for the remainder of her life, she rushed for the upstairs bedroom and drew a well-concealed pistol from her vanity drawer. What possessed the lady to arm herself, she had no clue. But the decision proved pertinent, as sounds of baying animals filled the home telling her that the raiders were attempting to confiscate the mules her husband had left on site.[98]

Rushing to the doorway, she was distraught to discover that the men who were depriving her property of its last four-legged animals were not clad in the blue wool of Union troopers. Instead, the wiry scarecrows were criminals disguised in the mute tones that had, until recently, been looked upon with kind eyes. Filling the air with squalls to cease their offenses immediately, her demands were met with utter indifference. Further protest, taking the form of a total rebuke of the troopers' reverence in the eyes of God, garnered the attention of one mischievous rider. Advancing on the front porch, he insisted that the Mrs. Steele grant him entrance into her home.[99]

Infuriated by the audacity of the demand and determined not to have a single floorboard of her abode polluted with the putrid filth of the trooper's boots, she refused in a very unbecoming manner. Although customarily meek, the lioness dug deep into darkness that dwelled inside her and found the constitution to produce the revolver she had tactfully concealed behind her back. The sudden armed confrontation took the trooper by surprise. Looking downward at the slender woman who leveled a rather large revolver at him, he initially tried to bully her into lowering her arm by confidently advancing with a stern step.[100]

The thud of his solitary aggressive step was answered with the sounds of a rotating cylinder as Mattie drew the hammer from its home, grasped the pistol with both hands and leveled it squarely at the head of the trooper, who stood at her mercy not five feet away. The barnyard quieted as the tense scene came to the attention of his comrades. Although looting was the order of the day, not a single one of them had devolved to an animal state cruel enough to cut down a young bride defending her hearth and home. Staring at the dark tube that housed what could be his doom, the aggressive trooper slowly backpedaled with hands raised to eye level in a sign of submission. While the morning's adventure had the potential to be lucrative, and the mules were certainly an adequate stopgap for their hoof-sore mounts, nothing to be found on the property was remotely important enough to risk springing a leak over.

Understanding that the moment had passed and resigned to leave the mules on the property, the troopers quickly began to undo what they had begun. While a few of the abortive thieves liberated the mules from leaders attached to their bridles, compatriots returned the implements that they had lifted from the barn. After returning the deadly minx's property, the troopers mounted with a nervous expedience that could only be derived from an embarrassing capitulation to the fairer sex.[101]

The specter of Wheeler's command haunted Steele for the next few days. Visited with startling regularity, the lone hellion always greeted her unwelcome guest with the same hospitality, defiantly standing in her doorway with a cocked and leveled pistol. Feminine defiance did not go unrewarded. Despite the odds, her property, including the prized saddle of a deceased brother, was left untouched. Standing down every gray rider who had the audacity to disgrace even the slop of her sty, the diminutive lioness became notorious for her wildness.[102]

Now, ten days out since the destruction of the Catawba River Bridge at Nations Ford and the slight looting of neighboring communities by rogue members, the entire division was once again nearing the border with South Carolina. It was there, traversing the hills of Rutherford County, that Palmer received the unexpected news that Davis was already well beyond Yorkville and dissecting the Piedmont in an apparent effort to reach the Savannah River. With this revelation, the Delawarean diverted the majority of his men due south and blazed the roads leading into the foothills that lay beyond the Blue Ridge, making their ultimate destination the transforming cotton junction of Spartanburg.[103]

The town, which had contributed an abnormally large percentage of its population to the cause of states' rights, continued its prosperous commerce through the war unencumbered. This peaceful streak, naturally, was about to be shattered. Prior to their long-dreaded entrance into Spartanburg, the First Brigade crossed into South Carolina to bed down. Following the highway that connected Spartanburg County with Rutherford County, a sense of poetic justice was felt at the selection of their campsite for the evening of April 29. By a twist of fate, the First Brigade bivouacked on the same soil where a southern army had cemented the inception of the Union way back in 1781: the old Cowpens battleground.[104]

Knowing that time was of the essence, Palmer surmised that the only plausible option that Davis had for freedom was to ford the Savannah River at Petersburg Crossing. Naturally, this would be undertaken in anticipation of finding sanctuary in Athens, Georgia. On tenterhooks with the intelligence that Davis's party would be slow moving, Palmer dispatched his beloved Fifteenth Pennsylvania in the direction of Abbeville. It now became their sole duty to scout the southernmost route that Davis could follow without threat of being intercepted by the copious numbers of troopers stationed in Charleston, taking full liberty to root the rat out of whatever nest it may have found refuge in.[105]

Unheralded, the arrival of the depleted brigade of two regiments into Spartanburg on April 30 was an early evening scene full of angst and dread for the local population. Arriving in Spartanburg during the five o'clock hour, the troopers surrounded and cut off the city. While the utmost attention was paid by the brigade provost to ensure that private property was respected, the printing press of the *Carolina Spartan* was befouled with their assistance. In an exercise of misunderstood humor administered by a regimental printer-turned-prankster, Sergeant Joe R. Lonabaugh, the Main Street offices of the publication were entered under the auspices of the provost guard.[106]

The extra, with type set by the capable hands of Lonabaugh, announced that the command had taken up residence in the town and that no private property was to be threatened. Instead, the Yankees were not the devils that the inhabitance had anticipated. Reflective of the Quaker State sergeant's personality, he humorously quipped that the spirit of Philadelphia would ring throughout the town. This display of wit, perhaps misunderstood by the fear-saturated population, netted the author a prestigious offer to dine with the editor of the paper he had commandeered and dinner visitations by notables of the municipality in appreciation of his soothing edition.[107]

The night that the First Brigade spent in Spartanburg was less than uneasy, as what would later be known as the Hub City of South Carolina received the most gentile visitation of the raid. While it is the definition of naivety to assume that not a single home was pilfered, there are no surviving records of animosity toward civilians conducted at the hands of the First Brigade that evening. Persuasion may have aided in the fair treatment of the inhabitants of Spartanburg, as Palmer later recounted that the inhabitants of Spartanburg could beg harder for the safeguards of their property than those in any other secessionist hole in the South.[108]

Fragmenting at the old battleground, the First Brigade simultaneously visited the town of Spartanburg while haunting both Spartanburg and Union Counties in search of information on Davis's whereabouts. Although many stories abound about trivial amounts of looting, most of which revolved around the abduction of livestock, little trauma was bestowed on the population by the raiders as they gathered intelligence. Knowing that Davis was employing the stagecoach roads that connected Yorkville with Abbeville, several of the raiders disturbed the southeastern extremes of the two counties.[109]

It was the cursory patrolling of these roads that brought the raid to its southeast terminus in South Carolina. Long in the tooth, a few raiders began to scavenge for food, fortune and mounts. Expanding their search to the nearest targets of opportunity, several of the raiders briefly penetrated the western confines of Chester County. Upon receiving word that Federal troopers were in the vicinity, the martial elderly and infirm decided to mobilize a scant militia force they had managed to construct.[110]

The gathering was the product of a good many wasted Saturday afternoons. Patriotic boosterism, ignorant in its folly, perpetuated the grand illusion that they would be able to effectively defend hearth and home in their feeble state—a delusion only made more solid by electing to saturate the soil of their community with the juvenile blood of sacrificial lambs. As word spread throughout Chester that the junior reserves were to be mobilized for a defense of the town, the mother of J.J. Hull called him from the earthen rows he was tending with a hoe and ordered him to make good his escape.[111]

Assembled in protest, the matrons of the yeoman community cackled together in panic at the prospect of their young sons being sent to the slaughter. Coming to the conclusion that a temporary exodus was the only acceptable option, the agitated hens agreed that the fruit of their clutch would depart before first light in order to avoid the lecherous hands of the local militia-mustering officer. Instructed to lead the family's only remaining livestock, a cow with a solitary horn and a lame horse stricken with equine gout, Hull was laden with a few days' rations and sent along with the entourage, seeking respite in the isolated forest near Dutch Fork.[112]

Progress was slow going, as the boys were overly cautious. Impeded by the burden of his lame horse, Hull soon lost pace with his accompaniment. Before long, his only company was a friend, Ephraim Able, who was more concerned with waging war on the blisters that populated his poorly shod feet than on the fabled invaders. Electing to take refuge in a dense pasture divide a few hundred yards from the roadway, the pair lay prone for the majority of two days in hopes of avoiding detection.[113]

Crashing back to the squalid world after relishing in the ecstasy of dream, the duo abandoned their subconscious desires. Arising unfulfilled moments before the debut of their second morning in a state of silent limbo, the ravenous juveniles discovered that their rations were depleted and their trousers tacky. Confronted with the uncomfortable sound of hollow stomachs for the first time in their lives, the youths elected to return to their homes and face the consequences that would accompany the pacification of their internal grumbling. Slowly progressing down the eerily deserted roadway, the boys returned home around dusk-dark.[114]

Settling their eyes upon a wasted matriarchy, it was clear that their adventure was in vain. Indeed, the panic felt in Chester had been an exaggerated case of war nerves and reckless bravado. The troopers had no intention of preying on Chester, and the youths who had heeded the call of the junior reserve were inconvenienced for a length of time shorter than Hull's dew-chilled discomforts of his first night in exile.[115]

While the First Brigade was busy with its adventures in the central and Eastern Piedmont, the two sister brigades departed Asheville on a cross-country sprint down the mountains. Descending the steep slope of Howard's Gap, the sight of their most recent engagement, the two brigades made swift and unopposed progress through the heart of the lawless Dark Corner. Bound for Anderson, many of the men were venturing across familiar territory, as the Dark Corner was inhabited by scores of loyalists and served as a noted refuge for opportunistic deserters of both sides. It was at that point that the command structure of the two Home Yankee brigades lost all semblance of order.[116]

In a dispatch addressed to the adjunct general of Stoneman's headquarters, Major Gustavus M. Bascom, General Palmer decried the state of Brown's and Miller's Brigades. Outraged at the behavior that had started in western North Carolina, the disgruntled general noted that the officers had lost complete control of their men and that the chief order of business was alleviating the local population, no matter what their social status, of their only valuable possessions. Drawing the wrath of Palmer in particular was General Simeon B. Brown, a man who had given his men carte blanche to exercise their tirade of pillage. Knowing that the worst was yet to come in the virgin hills of South Carolina, Palmer was right in his assumptions that the men not directly under his thumb were going to leave the population with a hatred of the uniform that would last for generations.[117]

The multilayered splintering of the command as it preyed on South Carolina was on par with the widespread fragmentation that Stoneman had undertaken in southwestern Virginia just a few weeks earlier. The raiders under Palmer burst into so many different directions that they appeared to be everywhere at once, leaving most townships and crossroads in the region with stories of visitation that were ritualistically recited by family elders countless times at the prodding of young Carolinians for whom the war was a romantically magic experience. While Palmer had released the Fifteenth Pennsylvania on an exhausting ride toward the Savannah River in hopes of rooting out Davis's location, the fragmentation of Brown's and Miller's Brigades might have been largely due to the disintegration of discipline rather than an effort to turn stones in search of the fugitive executive.[118]

With such widespread canvassing, the chronology of the raid once again becomes murky. Until the moment that the main column crossed the Savannah River into a smoldering Georgia, troopers were reported present in just about every locale in upstate South Carolina within the course of four days. As a single day witnessed reports of Palmer's men along the Savannah River, fragments of the First Brigade accompanied by renegades from Brown's command venturing as far south as Laurens County and Miller's Brigade battling junior reserves along the border of Anderson and Greenville Counties, the confused terror of the citizenry of the upstate of South Carolina was at its highest point of the entire war.[119]

While the two wings of Palmer's Brigade prepared to depart from Spartanburg County for points farther to the south and east, elements of Brown's brigade had miraculously covered a monumental amount of ground to somehow arrive in Laurens County. Having reversed course from their march northwest of Asheville on the morning of the twenty-eighth, various squads from Brown's Second Brigade began to trickle across the Enoree River on the evening of May 1. Visited by troopers who elected to spend

As the various armies traversed South Carolina soil, scenes like this were commonplace. *Courtesy of the Library of Congress.*

the evening in the outbuildings of the Boll Farm, the uneasy family was terrorized throughout the night in exchange for their unwilling hospitality. Stripping the farm of livestock and what minor valuables the small farming family possessed, the detachment of raiders completed their savagery with an action that was very uncharacteristic of the raiders: they torched the entire farm in front of the family.[120]

Under the guise of pursuing the renegade president, the troopers progressed deeper into Laurens County. Traveling to Hickory Tavern, the pack of wolves visited upon the crossroads the same treatment that had befallen the Boll family. Looting every residence that they crossed along Boyd's Mill and Erwin's Mill Roads, the troopers cast harm upon a backwater of the Confederacy that had yet to experience the direct inconvenience of the war. At the railroad town of Laurens, the depot and quartermaster stores were plundered with remarkable efficiency before the raiders departed, leaving the possessions of the townspeople relatively intact. Having successfully plucked the ripe cherry of Laurens County, the troopers crossed over into Anderson County by way of Erwin Mill Road.[121]

D. Sullivan Sr. remembered that the raiders arrived at his farm just a few days after he had returned to his wife from his tenure in the Army of Northern Virginia. As a veteran cavalry scout, Sullivan knew better than to challenge the multitude of repeating rifles and revolvers that were clutched by the home intruders. Sullivan, acknowledging the conditions of his parole, did not raise a finger and tried to maintain a ruse of cordiality toward the raiders. The end result of their visitation was that nine heads of stock were lost, including the heartbreaking pinch of his cavalry mount, which the bankrupt farmer had purchased a couple of seasons earlier for $125 in gold. In addition to the loss of his war horse, a coal black marsh tacky that the captain of his company had given to his little girls was taken by an unnamed colonel with the intention of bringing it back to Indiana as a present for his wife.[122]

Having been affronted by the raiders, the retired trooper waited for distance to develop between the thieves and his remaining property. After a restless night, Sullivan loaded the pistols that he kept in a secluded floorboard and began strolling down the road in search of stray mounts that gluttonous troopers had abandoned as finer specimens came into their possession. Having collected several mules feasting on roadside brambles, the scavenger was surprised by the deep brogue of a Scotsman. Slowly turning, Sullivan was face to face with an immigrant trooper who enlisted in Pittsburg and who now leveled his Spencer Carbine directly at the salvager's chest.[123]

This period sketch illustrated the idealized chivalric glory of the mounted soldier. In reality, the life of the trooper was exhausting and squalid at best. *Courtesy of the Library of Congress.*

Together, the pair rode down the Augusta Road, toward the direction of Honea Path, in search of pickets belonging to the rearguard. Fortunately for the captive, no such beast existed, as discipline had completely disappeared in the rear echelons and the troopers had marched off toward Anderson, having abandoned the Scotsman. Biding his time, Sullivan waited for the Scotsman to lower his guard. Disregarding the captive from his peripherals for only a second, the contractual pacifist was able to turn the tables on his captor, employing the revolvers that the wayward trooper had neglected to inspect for.[124]

Returning to Laurens County with twenty mules and a screaming banshee, the parole violator came across a squad of Wheeler's command. All too willing to be free of any evidence of his momentary lapse of adherence to the conditions of his parole, the amateur provost quickly surrendered his prisoner to the ragtag band. Unbeknownst to Sullivan, the very squad to which he handed his prisoner over had just that very morning, May 3, raided his neighbor's farm and stolen his horses. Upon receiving this information later in the afternoon, Sullivan tracked down the wayward Confederates and managed to negotiate a trade in mules for his neighbor's prized mount.[125]

While fragments from Brown's brigade were fording the Enoree in search of mischief, a sliver of Miller's command undertook a less fruitful experience in the northwestern confines of Greenville County. According to J.B. Lewis, a sixteen-year-old third sergeant who was naively mustered into service with the South Carolina Military Academy in the closing weeks of the war, his platoon of young lions ambushed a small detachment of troopers at an advantageous spot near Marietta around midday on April 30. With the loss of one digit on the hand of an unfortunate cadet, a wound dealt by a shotgun blast from the emancipated guide who was leading the raiders through the mountain coves of north Greenville, the affront was answered when an unnamed trooper was unseated by a musket ball loosed in the startling and efficient volley. Riding back to Greenville with the expectedly terrifying news that the raiders were near, the reunited cadet battalion abandoned the city at the bequest of local officials to take up positions along the Greenville and Columbia Railroad near Belton—a crossroads between Greenville and Anderson.[126]

As the cadets were quickly being schooled in the art of bushwhacking, the main body of Brown's and Miller's Brigades progressed down Jones Gap out of Transylvania County, North Carolina, and into Greenville County. Accompanying them was an additional company of 150 mounted infantry under Major James Lawson, which had been attached to the command at the bequest of General Davis Tillson. It was that company, deviating from the course of the two brigades that rode on to Pickensville, which visited Greenville on the night of April 30. The city was a nervous wreck in anticipation of what was to come, having been chosen as one of the many depositories to serve as a haven for the rich treasures of Charleston in hopes that they would survive the troubles intact.[127]

Local well-to-do, Carolina Gilman, remembered the entrance of the troopers into the city very well. Having just sat down to dinner with the rest of the household, the diners were roused by the sounds of screams and gunfire. Running to the veranda, the family witnessed in horror a local black man driving his wagon down their street in a mad panic, screaming at the top of his lungs that the Yankees were in town. No sooner had the former slave entered their view than a patrol of troopers came abreast of the wagon and forced the man from out at gunpoint. They then unhitched the wagon and rode out of view with the team.[128]

In a flash, the city of Greenville was inundated with lustful troopers. Houses were entered, and valuables departed the possession of countless families. Only at the home of Captain Wesley Brooks, however, did the troopers engage in malevolent destruction. Drunken troopers, who were slighted by the armed inhabitants who refused them entry, aborted a malicious attempt at arson after an uncooperative fire refused to spread. In addition to the looting of private treasures, the stores of local merchants were broken into and relieved of their valuable merchandise. Hungry for any specie that the raiders could lay their hands upon, the store of Hamlin Beattie was broken into and relieved of the $30,000 in currency he was concealing for the embattled Bank of Charleston.[129]

As the spirits that were uncovered from a local merchant's shop began to flow, the troopers engaged in an activity that resulted in demands for satisfaction from a few of the remaining men in the city. The marauders, driven by spite, flaunted the former possessions of the residents right in front of them. One unfortunate civilian attempted to avenge the insult by firing a shot in the direction of the troopers. Contrary to every cornerstone of his machismo-saturated upbringing, the outgunned chivalric hero was cut down right before his family's eyes.[130]

In addition to the murder of the hearth defender, a loyal slave was dispatched under dubious circumstances before he could experience the breath of freedom that the troopers were supposed to have granted him. Having picked the city of Greenville as clean as 150 efficient troopers could, the company departed the town that evening ahead of Palmer's men and rejoined the Second and Third Brigades on the road to Anderson. Arriving in the wake of the fiasco, the lightened First Brigade bedded down on the grounds of the Soldiers' Home and Female Academy. While no reports of looting survive from the second round of visitation, their welcome was severely cooled by the misbehavior of their predecessors.[131]

The detachment of cadets that had inaugurated the successful ambush at Marietta were less fruitful on the outskirts of Williamston. The boys, run ragged by an exertion of energy uncustomary to their youth, were gullible enough to fall for a ruse executed by an advance guard of troopers. In the darkness of the early morning hours of May 1, a handful of pickets from the cadet company were awoken by a series of shadowy mounted men who, with their thick mountain accents, claimed to be a detachment that had strayed from Wheeler's command and were trying to catch up with Jefferson Davis's faithful band. Allowing the company to pass unopposed, the early morning sky shimmered with fire to the south. In their tragic naivety, the cadets allowed the troopers to pass undetected in the darkness that shrouded the picket post, opening the road to the railroad stop and giving them unabated license to torch the junction.[132]

After ransacking the quartermaster stores that the cadets had hoped to draw from, both a freight and a passenger train were intercepted as they sat idle for the evening. Burning the former and forcing the inhabitants off the latter in order to fleece them, the troopers continued on their expedition toward Anderson. As with the confusing hysteria that surrounded the closing days of the war, when the cadets arrived, the remaining inhabitants of Williamston hid in fright. Believing the young men to be another column of United States soldiers, the lingering citizens who had not fled to the hillside failed to show themselves until after a few tense moments of convincing.[133]

A whirlwind of Federal troopers fostered widespread panic throughout the foothills of South Carolina in the closing days of April 1865. The momentary, albeit traumatic, visitation left an imprint on the upstate that has long been the foundation of regional folklore. Physically unaffected by the conflict, even though the emotional scars of war had long been felt, an image of blue riders marauding down the majority of the red clay back roads and paved thoroughfares left the population with a genuine sense of defeat—exactly the objective George Stoneman had hoped to achieve when he set out with his division in late March. With the exception of Spartanburg, which was spared the wrath of ravenous troopers due to the watchful eye of General Palmer, the raiders had done a satisfactory job of leaving no stone unturned in the boroughs that crossed their paths. Although much pain had been bestowed on the region by their malicious hands, the worst was yet to come as the sun rose on May Day, and Anderson waited in the distance.

3
"The Tennesseans in Their Present Condition Do Not Add Any Strength to the Union Forces"

Attempting to extract what little advantageous perspective the mediocre summit offered, Captain Landon Carter strained his eyes to make sense of the queer sight in the distance. Emerging from the crest of an opposing hill, Carter was in disbelief at the brood of martial ducklings that were advancing in his direction, a shy distance behind a demented drake and shrouded in the hazy byproduct of the mid-morning heat. "Damn it!" Instinctively cursing the poor visibility that the rolling hills of Anderson County had to offer while in the midst of their daily evaporation, the senior trooper wondered out loud, "What the in the hell is that?"

Puzzled by the rhetorical question, his close friend and messmate First Sergeant George W. Little entertained the misplaced musing by informing his friendly superior, "That's a line of infantry advancing." Continuing on with the perplexing conversation, he asked, "Should I order the boys to dismount and draw up a line?" It was at this point that Little's thick mountain twang surfaced: "There ain't that many. We may very well be able to drive 'em off and avoid the wait."[134]

Slightly annoyed at the genuine response to his verbal rumination, Carter killed the interaction by clarifying his interest with a chuckle. "God damn it George, I was talking about the flag those bastards are sporting!" Understanding the nature of the conundrum, the sergeant focused his eyes to the extent of their ability. After a few moments of digesting the curiosity that was rapidly closing on them, crossing into the pasture that laid itself out directly before them, Little issued his unsolicited opinion: "It's red, but it looks like their state flag." Upon a reassuring second observation, he added,

"Hell, I'm quite certain that it's the state flag." In a final moment of pointless contemplation, Little reflected, "That gaudy color sort of ruins the whole damn thing."

The inquisitive reflection was not to last long, as one constant that had escaped the helmsmen in their aesthetic inquiry was not lost on the enlisted raiders: the gray line was rapidly advancing toward their exposed and undeployed column. As the barking commands of the Confederate noncommissioned officers became clearly audible, Carter arrived at the realization that the entire company was in real and present danger. It was right then and there that the mesmerized captain crashed back into reality and arrived at the morning's watershed: should his troopers elect to fight at this late hour and risk the very real possibility of further devastating the coves of Tennessee with needless casualties, or should he withdraw his men tactfully in an effort to avoid conflict while saving face? Confronted with the real prospect of negligently adding sacrificial lambs to the smoldering pyre, Carter motioned to his subordinate with a silent nod, turning the ass of his mount to the Confederate advance in Spartan salute and placing spur to mount.

Tired of the martial charade and pissed that his advancement was interrupted by the unscarred naivety of amateur soldiers, Carter conceded the hillside for the well-being of his men. Trailing his men as they retreated to the shade afforded by a tree line crowning the next in a long series of hilly pastures, the disgruntled junior officer was brought to a sigh by the rude tenacity of his unrelenting adversary. Ashamed by his emasculating retreat, he sounded out in an uncustomarily deep baritone, "Column left!" As the dark hemisphere of the shaded morning grove began to cross the brim of his hat, a nervous twitch that danced across the shoulders of a trooper while his command resonated in the rider's ears was not lost in the glaring transition that blinded the captain. It goes without saying that the command haunted many of the disenchanted enlisted men, as if their officer had, for a brief moment, lost his mind. Turning his mount in an effort to face his company—which was resigned to the fact that the order to construct a line in an effort to make a stand was very real—as it filed past, his heart melted at the sullen faces that locked eyes with him. Determined not to lead his highland troopers to the narcissistic suicide in which his lowland counterparts had elected to indulge, Carter drew a large debt against his pride. "Re-form column along the roadbed." The words boomed from his sternum much to the surprise of his men, most of whom had assumed that the morning was going to offer one final reap for the death harvest. Content to withdraw his cadre to the next in an endless line of rolling hills, the captain hoped that the voluntary relinquishment would abate the appetite of the well-formed line that was incessantly gnawing away at whatever amount of distance Carter could afford his men.

The concession did not matter. As the minutes ticked by, the mid-morning air began to echo with commands hurled by rival line officers as they guided their infantrymen past the various obstructions that dotted the landscape. Young and invincible, the well-groomed lions continued their advance over the hillside and onto the opposing rise that the hospitable troopers occupied. Pressed beyond the acceptable point of courtesy, the crossroads where Carter and his detachment of the Eighth Tennessee gathered took on a grave symbolism.

Understanding that the mind of their aggressor was swayed decidedly toward bloodshed and that an exchange was to be forced upon them, Carter resigned himself to take action for the well-being of his men. Utilizing a subtle rise in the road, the company was strung along the meandering grade and instructed to rest in a prone position, taking advantage of a nervously brief respite amongst the sun-bleached straw that co-inhabited the future battle site. Deployed in a textbook skirmish formation, a thin frontline supported by a mounted reserve and a few troopers sequestered to protect the unoccupied mounts at the rear, the moment of truth was nigh.

The nested vipers, baking in the warm radiation of the late spring sun, were wholly on edge. Having participated in many of the larger campaigns of the region, the nervous energy of the mid-morning air was not lost on the men; a fatalism that could not be ignored saturated the rapidly dissipating haze. Like a terminally ill man destined to pass away in the few eternally dark seconds that transpired before his final day-clean, the troopers languished in their fleeting mortality. Carter, one of only a handful of fully erect combatants comprising the half-assed ambush, could see the toll that the weight of concern had on his men; many were fidgeting and distraught with the prospect that they were to be left cold with disappointment after flirting with the remote possibility that they would survive the conflict.

In only a few minutes, an uncomfortable silence crept across the field. As its diminutive inhabitants, sensing the direly uncomfortable situation, sought refuge in the countless sanctuaries that went unnoticed, the vanguard of the foolish Confederate advance came into view. At first the sea of straw danced in the breeze. It was the crimson rag that had prompted the morning's inquisitive observation, however, that impolitely broke the tranquility of the natural ballet.

Enraged by what was to follow, "Goddamn that imposing banner!" was the only imposition upon the silence that Carter could mutter, pretending, somehow, that if he kept quiet enough the Confederate advance would unsuspectingly press forward over the tops of his men and eventually over the horizon. The thought, however, was less directed toward the inanimate banner than at the reckless audacity of its pilot. The commander no doubt drove his untested amateurs toward the disenchanted veterans in a vain effort to garner a few laurels to fill his conversational repertoire following the war. Like many self-appointed local heroes, late-hour antics were necessary to make up for the fact that they were either too cowardly or too inept to serve in major theaters of combat, thus condemning the local hierarchy to be eternally, yet apathetically, entertained with years of pompous bullshit. This unbridled quest for heroic lip service was justified, since the majority of the region's young men had long since surrendered their lives for the perpetuation of cotton-picking fairy tales, leaving only impostors to fill the void created in their absence and pacify the legend-starved audiences of future generations.

Hunkering down in an effort to avoid exposing himself to undesired opportunism, Carter quietly signaled for his men to bring their Spencer carbines to the ready. Sweat beaded down more than one brow as the increasingly prominent sun filled the sky. Discouraging temptation to break form and relieve their faces of the moist tickling sensations, the nervous troopers occupied the uncomfortable final moments with sheepishly monotonous chants—all in an effort to guard their nerves from the obvious ill that was about to befall them. Naively, as the troopers settled in for their kill, the various field varmints began to surface from the previous year's straw, entirely oblivious to the burden of heavy metal that the air was about to shoulder. It was at that precise moment that the moral dilemma of the morning presented itself: to engage in orchestrated murder by opening upon the unsuspecting youths or withdraw to yet another hilltop?

Unwary, this small fragment of the Corp of Cadets came into full view. Staring directly into their virgin eyes, totally uncorrupted by the psychologically disabling specter of war, Carter was instantly sickened by the prospects of the massacre that the simple swipe of his hand could set into motion. "I can't do this," he decided. The sighing conclusion to the morning's retreat extracted every ounce of hatred from the captain as he reflected, "They may be unrelenting bastards—but for Christ's sake—they are just kids." It was at that point that Landon Carter resigned himself to what had to be done.

Encroaching on the closest ear of a nervously twitching bushwhacker, he whispered an unexpected stratagem, "Pass it down: the first three rounds go over their heads." A fluttering oculus, tinted brown by the diluted bloodshot of a daily morning hangover, expanded at news of the surprising benevolence. This primal reflex was indication enough for the captain to know that the message was fully understood and that word would silently trickle down his entire line. In just a matter of seconds, the repetitious jerk of heads in the direction of Carter was indication enough that the order had made it down the length of the line unadulterated. Slightly raising his hand, in an effort to keep below the crown of the neglected winter's straw, the benign executioner waited for the moment of truth to arrive.

The juvenile assaulters were loud and negligent, an amateur misstep that diminished the sight of their impressively pristine battle line. Their spectacular demonstration, the zenith of a solid military education, was useless pageantry in the face of deadly laymen who had long grown accustomed to the smell of lead penetrating the hollow chests of their social betters. Unlike the countless ambushes that Carter and his men had performed in the past, for once, the freefall of his hand under a timid force led to a philanthropic volley.

As a broadside perforated the air high over their heads, the splendid martial recital plummeted for the earth without directive. Aerating the spring dust with the forceful imprint of their buttons was entirely foreign to such a splendid collection of youths, many of whom had devoted the majority of their wartime experience to drill; that was, of course, when they were not sadistically taunting the prisoners under their care. Recovering from their momentary lapse in chivalry, the cadet company wildly opened up on the hidden raiders with an undisciplined volley that would have embarrassed even the most fair-weather of militiamen. As the cold blue steel of the Massachusetts stamped levers made their triple repetition, the captain was rattled by knowledge that subsequent ejections were to be well homed.[135]

"Fall back to the mounts!" The command took even the most adamant proponents of self-preservation by surprise. Knowing full well that the distraught line of Confederate home guard were outgunned and already longing for the safety of the opposing ridgeline, the notion that Carter would order a retreat in the face of triumph was, at the very least, unanticipated. Although versed in the superiority of their position, the underlying nature of the order was not lost on the troopers: the war was over, and a well-covered retreat was in everybody's best interest.

Instantaneously, the remaining three or four rounds were expelled from their repeaters without guidance. Bursting forth from the pediment of the undergrowth like a geyser, the entire skirmish line bolted for the defilade. Employing the opportunistic safety that was afforded them by the inexperience of their adversaries, the entire detail reached the timber intact; all the while, their unyielding antagonist occupied the confusing moment by wildly attempting to drive half-poured cartridges down the barrels of their muzzleloaders.

The retreat was hot and hectic, as not a single trooper desired to be a finalist for the title of "last man killed in the war." Penetrating the tree line in an episode of unprecedented invulnerability, not a single percussion cap was inconvenienced by the impact of a cadet's hammer, as the entire student body was timidly loading their pieces after experiencing a hostile welcome for the first time in their careers. Tearing their pants on the briars that hugged the hardwoods constituting a thin divide between cleared lands, winded troopers were welcomed by the sight of their waiting mounts.

Warming many a worn felt hat with radiant sunlight as the last few saplings of the tree line were passed and the wayfaring troopers reunited with their estranged mounts, celebratory uncouthness caressed the troopers' ears from the distance. Ignorant as to the stay afforded them, young cadets from The Citadel were enthusiastically celebrating the benevolent retreat of the Tennesseans. Unaware that the vast majority of the company could have been sliced clear through in a manner that was eerily reminiscent of the first ignorant souls to follow a false idol toward a prone skirmish line in 1861, joyous yelps glazed over any suspicion of how close death had actually stood to the toy soldiers.

The injustice, however, would have to stand. Content that he was paired against fools, Carter ordered his men to withdraw farther to the rear, resigning himself to avoiding casualties at all cost. Considering the unacceptable toll that a general row would have taken, it was the only clear choice. For the remainder of his life, as the engagement was touted as the last Confederate victory east of the Mississippi River in some circles, Carter could take solace in the unsung satisfaction that he had saved many men from unneeded sacrifice that morning.

This series of generous concessions made by the raiders to avoid a full-blown clash west of Williamston, South Carolina, are indeed considered the last successful Confederate attacks east of the Mississippi River in some circles, despite the fact that a large collection of local historical societies have also laid claim to this notoriously tragic achievement. Although the exact location of the martial game of chicken is unknown, many have placed it within earshot of the Patterson Mill that once resided outside Pendleton. In spite of its dubious background, the eruption that is still largely touted by locals of Anderson County and the South Carolina Military Academy as a

An illustration of the celebrated end result of planter-class aristocracy education that was the South Carolina Military Academy long before members of its student body elected to make a stand west of Williamston. *Courtesy of the Library of Congress.*

prime example of patriots defending home and hearth, is notable for one reason: the date the conundrum unfolded. Even though members of the Battalion of State Cadets were successful in reversing the course of a small and unidentified contingent of raiders, the majority of the Federal column passed through unopposed and advanced toward a destructive visitation on Anderson, reserving the empowering historical scrap a special place in the hearts of the local population, as it was the only shining moment in the darkness that was May 1, 1865.[136]

The arrival of that fateful day signed a solemn black spot on the annals of Southern history. As the sun cast its first rays on the hills of Anderson County, so too dawned the final month of the Southern nation. The next few weeks witnessed the remaining warm embers of the Confederacy being extinguished forever, as the small, determined enclaves of resistance withered and died almost simultaneously. While sporadic engagements were waged on both sides of the Mississippi River, many of which were decided in favor of the Rebel armies, all hope was lost for a legitimate continuation of the Southern effort. For generations after the fact, a plethora of dusty crossroads in just about every region of the South laid claim to being host to the last genuine engagement of the war. While this honor most likely belongs to Palmito Ranch, Texas, the sleepy town of Pendleton, South Carolina, petitioned its claim for the dubious distinction for many decades following the end of hostilities.[137]

Aside from the nearby engagement west of Williamston, apparently there were a few more flashpoints that erupted throughout that ominous morning. Closer to Pendleton, local home guard, a cradle-to-grave collection of young teens and gnarled men, took up the example established by the Battalion of State Cadets and elected to stand their ground. Caught off guard by the saturation of troopers throughout the county, the small company clashed with the advance guard of Simeon Brown's command near the Pendleton Factory.[138]

According to tradition, the fight was impromptu, lasting for only a few brief and surprisingly one-sided exchanges. Typical of the nature of worrisome gossip, news that the Federal troopers had advanced into the upstate of South Carolina spread fast. Made uneasy by the developments, community elders decided to take action. According to plan, local militias were mobilizing at the prearranged rallying points throughout the communities of Anderson. At one particular encampment, a collection of about two dozen militiamen were mulling around in a field awaiting the orders of the day. Anticipating that the group would have to travel countless miles to take up a position that would bring them into contact with the troopers, nervous conversation filled the air about what the day had in store for them. Chance, however, had other designs.[139]

It was at that very moment that a scout from a nearby detachment of the raiders rode into view. Totally ignorant to the presence of the home guard, the rider closed in on the rabble, perhaps blinded to the location of the gang by high grass or some other natural impediment. The end result was an unfortunate meeting that neither side anticipated nor desired.

Of the two belligerents, it was the collection of local invalids who fell under the command of First Lieutenant James Hunter that noticed their adversary first. Staring in disbelief at the rider who was nonchalantly trotting directly toward them, Hunter drew his men into a firing line and ordered his motley crew to bring their muskets to the ready. No sooner had the firing detail formed its line than the wayward rider discovered the gravity of his situation. Coming face to face with the small collection of amateur soldiers, the trooper halted, frozen in his tracks.

The solitary rider, unsuspectingly finding himself in a standoff with the gathering of mismatched men, demonstrated an unimaginable level of bravado. Saturated to the core with a surprise-induced adrenaline rush, the unnamed trooper flipped his brain like a card index for any action that might give him an advantage and allow him to make good his escape. With his carbine already resting on his hip, the outnumbered rider elevated it beyond the perked ears of his mount and let loose a lone round into the empty air. The waste of a government-issued cartridge was most likely an unspoken effort to either convince the militiamen to disband their cadre or, at the most charitable of his nature, inaugurate a parley with the unexpected foes.[140]

Nevertheless, his true intentions were never known. Before the outnumbered rider could bring his carbine down from its unnaturally elevated position and chamber an additional round, his fate was sealed. The motley crew responded with a well-regulated volley, which felled the man from his mount. Lifted from the saddle by the impact of two balls, his ears were filled with the tormented bays of a wounded mount just before he crashed into the dry May soil. Although the wounds were found to be superficial upon immediate inspection of his torso, the trooper's number was surely up.[141]

Hearing the sound of the militia officer ordering his men to reload and advance upon their prey, the trooper frantically searched the high grass for his carbine. Rifling through the interwoven mixture of dry stalks and spring greenery, the object of his desire was nowhere to be found. Lost in the miniature jungle of the untended Carolina field, the soldier drew his pistol in a fatally mismatched protest. Content to make the long straw his Alamo, like so many fellow Appalachians of his grandfather's generation who had succumbed to overwhelming odds in a burned-out mission of like name, the trooper rolled his aching body into the prone position and unseated the hammer.

Even though the trooper demonstrated his resignation to the fate that awaited him by readying his sidearm, the deities had other designs for the vigilant rider. As the shots echoed throughout the rolling hills, his comrades-in-arms picked up their pace in order to come to the assistance of their recklessly distant scout. In just a matter of seconds, more raiders rode into the clearing. Instantly seeing that time was of the essence, the troopers remained mounted, drew up a line of battle and charged headlong toward the militiamen with repeaters blaring.[142]

Expecting a crashing impact from the thundering mounts, the militiamen re-formed their lines just a few yards shy of their fallen victim and braced for the blow. However, the glorious charge was not to be. Coming abreast of the embattled trooper, the men drew up their reins and dismounted. Under the cover of a few talkative Spencers, an ambulatory team lifted their wounded comrade from the ground and threw him across the back of a mount with a rider at the ready.[143]

After the punctured soldier and wounded mount were recovered, the troopers withdrew to the tree line. In a few minutes, a rider crossed the pasture under a flag of truce. Informing the home guard that the true intention of the advance was only to pursue the renegade president and that the detachment had been ordered not to engage unless a dire situation developed, the home guard stood down. At that moment, the commander of the local militia, First Lieutenant James Hunter, allowed the Federals to cross their lines unopposed and ride onto Anderson, much to his everlasting regret.[144]

Although sometimes confused in local history with the clash near Patterson's Mill, the oral tradition of the skirmish greatly differs from well-documented accounts of the engagement just a short distance away. While the Confederate participants of the minor scrape boasted a solitary Union casualty as laurels, oddly enough, there was no mention made of the occurrence by the recipients of the defeat. In contrast, the bloodless exchange west of Williamston was acknowledged by both sides. A large component of its notoriety was the role of The Citadel in the clash and the school's claim that it was the final time the Battalion of State Cadets took the field in battle.

It was also the young participants who later insisted that they did not advance against the raiders but instead were swarmed as they slept under arms. As the institution remembered, they initially fell back but eventually rallied around their banner and drove the raiders from camp. This glaring contradiction of period sources is perhaps a sign of confusion with the nighttime ruse of the raiders east of Williamston, as the fog of time muddied the lines between the deception of the cadets and their redemption in the bloodless engagement.[145]

While Hunter's men were locked in an engagement ten miles northwest of Anderson, a third and almost simultaneous engagement transpired seventeen miles northeast of Anderson. Having fallen back from their compromised position at Williamston, the cadet company that had unknowingly allowed the troopers through the previous night now found themselves under the leadership of Colonel Thomas. Throughout the morning, their band had grown, and they were now accompanied by a small detachment of elderly home guard under Lieutenant W.P. Price. While attempting to rally and gather any details concerning the rapidly deteriorating situation, word arrived that troopers had been spotted only a little way down the road and were looting homes.[146]

Wasting no time, the reinforced company struck out under the auspices of Thomas and sought the morning's contest. Less than a mile or two down the dusty byway, the foot soldiers happened upon an isolated detachment of troopers that had encroached on the home of Thomas Moore near the village of Piedmont. Spreading out into squad-level fragments, the band somehow avoided detection as it silently inched toward the unsuspecting raiders, most of whom busied themselves with their greedy avocation inside the structures of the property. Drawing a bead on the few thieves who stood watch over the horses, a salvo unleashed by the local bushwhackers startled the property's unwelcome guests.[147]

The sudden announcement of the engagement rattled the troopers, who bolted from the house and outbuildings in a desperate effort to secure an expedient escape that only their mounts could offer. Clambering for any respite from the indiscriminate missiles, the yard was littered with a plethora of discarded valuables whose abduction had not even lasted long enough for the troopers to properly secure them in their haversacks. After exchanging a few rounds with their wily aggressors, the unruly marauders skedaddled, leaving a solitary wounded man behind. Closing in on their prize, it was evident that the soldier was severely wounded. Not inclined to instill more harm on the home's inhabitants, the wounded Federal was taken with the band as it withdrew.[148]

Collecting the injured raider, preparations were made to move him in the direction of Anderson for medical assistance. While nothing was said about his condition or his fate, it is most likely that he was either taken to the home of an anonymous resident or suffered the longer trip into the town proper. With their bellicose appetite extinguished by the morning's excitement, the entire band withdrew to a secluded spot to await further orders. It was there, in the hours following the engagement, that the collection of smooth-faced adolescents and gray-haired men elected to disband. Coming to the realization that their actions were perhaps doing more harm than good, all agreed that it would be in the community's best interest if they disarmed and went their separate ways in hope of remaining incognito.[149]

With roads laid wide open to the largest untouched population inhabiting the South Carolina side of the Savannah River, the troopers' blood was boiling due to the audacity of a local defense force that had yet to truly experience the horrors of war. Having done the Secession State justice in the ferocity of their actions, the raiders had yet to exhaust their penchant for misbehavior. As raiders approached the town limits of Anderson, many inhabitants had left themselves foolishly open to offense. The afternoon in question, May 1, was reserved for festivities in spite of the stories of hardship trickling in from the surrounding hillside. For the inhabitants of Anderson, the day in question was May Day, and their annual celebrations would not be smudged by rumors of advancing Federal riders.[150]

On this particular Monday, the local boarding school populations, many of whom had sought refuge along with their parents in Anderson from the protracted siege of Charleston, had elected to pass the holiday by holding picnics at various points throughout the greenery that surrounded the town. While the intention of the day was that of goodwill and fellowship, it was not to be. Although originally ignoring the rumors, word began to spread fast that there was Federal cavalry in the area and that minor skirmishes were dotting the countryside. Understanding that the danger was very real, the festivities were swiftly abandoned as participants fled for refuge. No sooner had most of the participants made it home, or even been made aware of the dangers that the day held, than troopers stormed into town from the north.[151]

Within a matter of moments, just as in every unarmed town on which the command had descended, Anderson was spewing troopers from every alleyway and thoroughfare. Firing their repeaters and sidearms into the air as screaming inhabitants scampered for cover, the unruly troopers of the Second and Third Brigades wasted no time in inaugurating their pillage. Although Simeon Brown had been promoted to overall commander of both brigades just two days before, subordinate only to William J. Palmer, Edwin M. Stanton and George Stoneman, the newly established chief did little to quell the behavior of his column. Everywhere one looked, there were troopers entering homes and leveling revolvers at cornered citizens, interrogating the frightened masses for the location of their valuables and alcohol.[152]

As the infestation spread, and viewing the intruders' actions as a violation of the peace signed between Ulysses S. Grant and Robert E. Lee, a few of the paroled Confederates attempted to engage the troopers in order to protect their own hearths. McKenzie Parker, an artillerist who had served in various theaters east of the mountains, quickly placed a weathered cap on his aging deer rifle and rushed into the yard to address the actions of the unruly men who were roving in front of it. Leveling his piece at a shadowy soldier, Parker ordered the thief to cast his weapons to the ground and to slowly dismount.[153]

Startled by the daring of the brazen homeowner, the audacious Union veteran leveled his carbine at Parker and demanded the same in turn. As wide eyes informed the beguiled of the upswing of the Spencer repeater, Parker fired. The heart-shattering snap of a foul cap was all that informed his senses of the effort. Drawing the hammer back again, frantically abandoning his aim for any hope of experiencing a belated recall, Parker fired once more.[154]

The only sensation that engrossed his senses was not the sharp recoil of a familiar rifle but the queer bite of a fifty-two-caliber lead slug tearing through his chest and drawing a small portion of his lungs through a gaping exit wound. Instantly, the world was consumed with lucid sobriety as the dispatched conducted a wide-eyed and fleeting inventory of his surroundings that seemed to go on for ages. As the luminous survey began to blur, Parker collapsed to the ground. Rushing into the fray, his family took hold of their vanquished champion and dragged the limp warrior back inside. While the troopers ransacked the terminal man's house, the inevitable ensued, and Parker died shortly after darkening his own door for the final time amidst the painful confusion that he had lost his life trying to prevent.[155]

Parker's death was not the only instance of violence toward the citizenry that day. In the midst of instructing an aspiring musician in the harmonious art, Caroline Ravenel was interrupted from her euphoria by the screams of children as a pair of local offspring burst in and was entirely unnerved by their claims that the troopers had fired on them. Jolting toward the window, the instructor arrived just in time to notice a local black package boy split across the head with a saber by an out-of-control trooper, who turned and fired his pistol into her yard. While violence was a common thread throughout the raid, the actions taken at Anderson began to border on the sadistic—a clear sign that the troopers themselves knew that the war was winding down and opportunities to extract financial acumen from the Southern population were nearing an end.[156]

Knowing that time was of the essence, the troopers became quite innovative in their development of diabolical methods of interrogation. While beatings and faux firing squads had been commonplace for some time, the introduction of hangings was most troublesome. Instead of a full-fledged lynching, however, the offended were strung up by an upward extremity until only the tips of their toes maintained contact with the earth and then slightly lifted off the ground in hopes that the agonizingly burdensome weight of their own body would encourage the divulgence of their valuables. The end result of the sadistic exercise was a veritable Appalachian strappado, which accumulated a long list of victims in a relatively short amount of time.[157]

Mr. Myers was hung with a rope tied around his neck, the opposite end of which was anchored to a tree outside his house. Beaten in the face with infuriated fists and left for dead, the offenders were unable to extract the location of a hidden alcove that held his gold. After Dr. Carter's home was destroyed in search of the elusive metal, the unfortunate physician was met by a similar fate. Having been strung up by his thumbs, the elder practitioner was left with a crippling injury that haunted him for the remainder of his life.[158]

At the home of Dr. Henry Ravenel, a most gruesome scene unfolded. Dr. Henry Winthrop, an elderly guest of the lady of the house, was strung up in an upstairs bedroom and beaten unmercifully with the flat part of a shovel. Believing that a large quantity of treasure rested at some point on the property, the community elder did his best to resist until his head was thrust into a wall and afterward threatened with execution. The sadistic integration was ultimately a success, as eventually the doctor divulged the location of a cubbyhole that contained a communal collection of treasures. While these isolated incidents were productive for the offenders, history is lost to the scores of victims who met similar fates and whose ordeals went unrecorded.[159]

Anderson, fully populated with troopers and picked clean by nightfall on May 1, was not an isolated island of torment surrounded by a sea of tranquility. The golden meadowlands of the countryside also suffered greatly at the hands of Brown's and Miller's men. At the home of Emmala Reed, daughter of the mayor of Anderson, a trooper with a volcanic temper arrived mid-morning on the first. Threatening to kill the men harbored in the house, the rider slung curses at the locked door until finally drawing his sword and decapitating the top of a gatepost.[160]

The unexpected vandalism was a bad omen for the family; in a flash, mounted men were swarming the yard. Bursting into the house, bandits lifted a shotgun, two revolvers, a jug of liquor and countless valuable bric-a-brac that had caught the eyes of the troopers. In the midst of the chaos, one audacious private took the insulting liberty of helping himself to the male inhabitant's toiletries in an effort to engineer a dapper appearance. Following this unfortunate tour of the home's inner sanctums, the family was taken downstairs.[161]

It was at that point that the offenders took the male inhabitants as prisoners, including an amputee wounded in the Army of Northern Virginia, with the intention of storing the enlisted men at the local courthouse and sending the officers on to Tennessee. However, these threats were more than likely a ruse to draw the local male population away from their homes since not a single former soldier was sent out of Anderson County. Fearing the worst, the orphaned females were subject to harassment by a constant stream of unwanted blue visitors. In a short time, the men of the house returned with a Federal officer, who had taken pity on the sight of the captive amputee and released the entire lot.[162]

Establishing a guard at the house, over the next few days Ms. Reed commented on the guard posts' kindness as she had obviously captured the eye of more than one of the raiders. The gifts of wine and alcohol that the smitten pillagers had brought, all of which were the former property of their less fortunate neighbors, gave a comforting air of cordialness to the nights the detail passed within their house. In an effort to exploit the newfound generosity, Ms. Reed's father used his clout as mayor to arrange guards for many of the well-to-do families of the town. The newfound sense of cordial security was not to last, as with the departure of the guard the ravenous troopers returned, at one point reliving the barn of its remaining bales of fodder and later relieving the family of their carriage and suitable mounts.[163]

Ms. Reed's diary made an inventory of the hardships experienced by other locals as well. The Boyle family was relieved of its horses, arms, patriarch's watch and vegetable garden's produce. Mr. Brown's home, which happened to be situated along the northeastern picket post, was continuously inhabited by the troopers. Stripped of all its furnishings and valuables before the command departed, the Brown residence was left stark naked in the wake of the raiders' tenure. Closer to Anderson, the Ruccor household was devastated by the blue-clad thieves, with troopers going so far as to mutilate the furniture before they departed.[164]

While Brown's and Miller's men were to blame for much of the devastation, Palmer's First Brigade was not without its offenses. At the home of Elias Earle, a well-to-do man who lived between Greenville and Anderson, the two regiments that remained with Palmer bedded down for the night. While Palmer and his staff rested inside the main house at the expense of the family's hospitality and fineries, the men of the Twelfth Michigan and Tenth Ohio were left to roam free on the property unencumbered. In a matter of hours, any item worth lifting from the family outside the house was spoken for.[165]

The first possessions to be filched were the slaves. Their bonds were not severed in the name of emancipation but because they were privy to the location of local valuables. Lifting the human livestock from their owners did not go unrewarded, as the servants quickly divulged the location of the family's swag. When the raiders' appetite was not pacified by the small bundles of jewelry that were uncovered, they began to deafen the ladies of the house by firing pistols over their heads in an effort to extract further troves.[166]

When the waste of ammunition failed, Preston Earle was dragged from the house and threatened with hanging. Brought to a tree that towered over his front yard, a rope was placed securely around his neck. The action did not sway Preston, as he was already resigned to his fate. In an act of reckless disregard for the well-being of his family, or perhaps the result of a clever evaluation of the constitution of his tormentors, Earle challenged his tormenters to burn down the house as they would not receive another cent from his family.[167]

Checked by their victim's insolence, the raiders turned their disappointed attention to the barn. Attempting to save face after their capitulation in the test of will, the raiders cherry-picked the livestock for suitable mounts. In an action that bordered less on charity than on necessity, the command's depleted mounts were left on the property. This unintended benevolence did much to keep the family's head above water in the hard months that followed, as the emaciated skeletons were of irreplaceable value for the local population during the upcoming agricultural season.[168]

As the sun hung low in the sky, the destruction of the holiday was devastatingly incomplete. It was this evening that the darkest fears of the townspeople were realized, as the massive store of liquor being concealed by a Mr. Guardine was broken into. The discovery of this secret crypt of ambrosia was the result of inadvertent political betrayal, as Anderson's mayor had divulged the location of the spirits earlier that day to Brown while engaged in idle conversation. No sooner had the sun retreated back behind the western horizon than a multitude of thirsty troopers poured into the building and quickly liquidated over $200,000 worth of stock in fine wine and spirits. The drunken revelry that ensued left officers of both brigades with the gargantuan task of bringing the intoxicated mob back to order.[169]

Fortunately for Anderson, the inebriation of the soldiers was grounded in joyous spirit. Elated by the day's fruits and the rapidly closing war, their drunken misbehavior did not transform into surly vengeance. While many storehouses were broken into and shop fronts defiled, the town was spared the erratic torch of the drunkards. In due time, after word spread that the stock had been depleted, a patrol arrived to herd the drunken soldiers back to camp—a vague bivouac, devoid of any order, that spilled over from the green spaces of the town and into its outskirts.[170]

In just a matter of hours, the sun crept into the opposite horizon and harkened the arrival of the second day of the terrifying occupation. After the troops roused, those who still remained attached to the frail cords of discipline assembled for roll call and received their orders for the day. The tasks at hand were destructively pleasant to the ears of the recipients: render the depot useless and waste the quartermaster stores in town. In short order, the stores were ransacked, and supplies critical to the command for their continued push toward the Savannah River were issued. Afterward, the remainder was cast into the streets for the local poor whites and emancipated blacks to scavenge through while the troopers busied themselves with their destructive duty. In due time, the depot was vandalized beyond timely repair.[171]

Throughout the morning of May 2, the pillage continued, including the infamous aborted hanging of Dr. Winthrop at the Ravenel House. With Palmer's Brigade passing through the vicinity, the orgy of pilferage came to an end. Ordering their brigades to mount up, Brown and Miller departed Anderson by four o'clock that afternoon. As they elected to take a road to the southwest in the direction of Augusta, while their increasingly impatient division commander took a more direct route to the Savannah River, the borderland was inundated with blue riders.[172]

While the main columns rapidly progressed toward the Georgia border, the local population was not quite in the clear. The rearguards of all three brigades continued the looting once they were beyond the all-seeing eyes of their commanders. However, by sunup on May 3, the rogue troopers had abandoned the town of Anderson out of fear. Knowing that distance between comrades in hostile territory could be the kiss of death, they rode out for the Savannah River.

This sudden departure was all too necessary to avoid any roving Confederate cavalry that might have shadowed the column into Anderson. It took no stretch of the imagination to understand that as the hours ticked by, their chances of a clean break greatly diminished; although, in this late hour, the dwindling bands of gray riders were less concerned with taking prisoners than picking through the scraps of civilian property that were left by the troopers. However, their presence meant trouble nonetheless.[173]

As they rode toward the still waters of the border, Palmer reflected on the damage that he had surveyed in the wake of Brown's and Miller's Brigades. The devastation was beyond anything that the Delawarean had ever imagined by the hands of faithful followers of the grand old flag. Although the First Brigade had engaged in many notable instances of pillage, the exhausted troopers still obediently followed orders, and their lust for plunder was easily quelled. However, doubts were beginning to ferment in the general's mind as to the validity of his subordinate brigade commanders' authority.[174]

If their commands were too far-gone to rein in, then their usefulness in the pursuit was void, and disciplinary action would have to be taken. The only question was when to initiate reform and to what degree. Should the pair fail to curtail their marauding men, then the First Brigade would be forced to continue its chase alone, and the War Department would have to be notified of the court-martial-worthy offenses. As the command crossed the river, Palmer decided his strategy. He would give his sister brigades the benefit of the doubt and withhold punitive measures until their arrival in Athens, Georgia.

4
"If You Can Hear of Davis, Follow Him to the Ends of the Earth, if Possible, and Never Give Him Up"

He is mad." Struggling to maintain the illusion of contemplative interest, the dumbfounded colonel gnawed away at the back of an inconspicuously tucked lip with his left incisor as the director of the meeting continued his introduction. The mood that filtered through the dining room of the Burt Mansion was strong with disbelief and diluted shock. It was slightly after four o'clock in the afternoon on May 2, and the long shadows of the evening began to slowly commence their silent creep across the corners of the room. Without muttering a word, five of the senior-most officers remaining in the skeletal Confederate army were listening in earnest to their commander in chief.[175]

In the speaker's mind, the room was filled with a veritable who's-who of the Confederacy's most loyal heroes, although the unfiltered reality of the assembly painted a different picture. Jefferson Davis, with sullenly exhausted eyes that betrayed his true physical condition despite his attempts to preserve a strong face, sat at the head of the table. Former United States vice president, Confederate secretary of war and current brigadier general John C. Breckenridge reclined in his chair to the left of the president, captivating Davis's full attention. The senior-most officer in the room, Lieutenant General Braxton Bragg, was masked behind the darkness of Davis's blind eye as he listened to the rant of his old ally.

Casting his one operational cornea out onto the room, the blurry image was a catastrophic change from meetings held just two months earlier. Rounding out the roll call of the final war council of the Confederacy were not the historic personalities with whom the president had become accustomed to conversing. Instead, a handful of brigadier generals—Samuel W. Ferguson, John C. Vaughn, George G. Dibrell and Basil W. Duke—and a diminutive colonel by the name of William C.P. Breckenridge were the only faces that stared back at the crippled politico. While Davis continued his assessment of the disheartening military situation, it was the least-tenured officer who was most taken aback by what the delusional executive was babbling.[176]

"One hundred thousand soldiers under arms in a few weeks," the muscles in the colonel's face were stressed beyond their elasticity *and* a grimace slowly crept across his face, "even if such numbers still breathed in this part of the country, we could never get them back into the field after so many paroles and furloughs." Sighing as the thought continued to weave, he added, "Hell, our provost could not even keep them in the field when we had them under our thumb to begin with." Portentousness climaxed as the president insisted that the war was far from over, and their flight through South Carolina was not an exodus but merely a strategic retreat to a stronger position. Throwing all of his faith in the triviality that John Bell Hood was dragging his twisted body toward Texas with the intention of rallying the western departments and taking command of the theoretical thirty thousand men still under arms in the Lone Star State, the war was anything but over in Davis's mind. In the aging Mississippian's eye, after a few miraculous reversals that the Southern armies were notoriously capable of producing, the Union tide would break, and the Confederacy could be resurrected one state at a time.[177]

Espousing every slogan, anecdote and homily that had been ingrained in the politician's memory, Jefferson Davis did his best to spark any semblance of patriotic fire that may have been smoldering in the Confederacy's remaining general officers. Having exhausted his voice to a raspy whisper, the president opened the table to comments from the officers. The table was quiet for some time as the subordinates stared at one another in near disbelief. Having fully expected that the afternoon's order of business was to come to a consensus over what steps should be taken to ensure the fugitive president's safety and a peaceful conclusion to the already dead war, Colonel Breckenridge spoke up first in an effort to cut through the tension.[178]

Releasing a very humbling sigh in an attempt to douse the fire stoked inside his belly at the thought of continued bloodshed in the name of the dead philosophy, the retort was barely audible as the colonel cast his gaze upon the clasped hands that covered the few unhinged buttons of his uniform coat. "Rally sir?" After the safety valve of subordination burst, the truth flowed from the insignificant officer like a tidal wave: "The country was decidedly lost in April, and there is nothing left to rally." The look upon the flustered executive's face was that of puzzled bewilderment as his head tilted slightly, absorbing the unexpected retort. "The situation that we find ourselves in, Mr. President, is hopeless." Mustering the courage to direct his eyes toward the gaunt face of the heartbroken idealist, he finished, "In my humble opinion all is lost." At that point, a chill filled the room, as the only sounds that cut through the tension were the echoes of light steps in the adjoining rooms and the gruff rumble of deep breathing that filled the chamber.[179]

After a few moments of icy glares exchanged between the two bookends of rank, Colonel Breckenridge broke from the contest of will and continued his critique without the uncomfortable burden of locking eyes with his superior. "Sir the situation is unsustainable. There is no base of supply, no hope for reestablishing one, nary a depot that has not been sabotaged and not a single safe harbor in which to reestablish a manufacturing base or construct an apparatus for the recruiting effort that you speak of." Battling away the shuddering sensation that rocked his shoulders, the chastised colonel finally developed the courage to espouse the obvious. "In lesser words, we are fugitives."[180]

With flush cheeks, dyed red as a result of unbridled loathing, the fuming president challenged the assumption of the lowly officer: "Colonel Breckenridge, if this were indeed the situation, then why do these brigades, particularly the men under your command, still ride on with me?" Coming to the full realization that the politician had begun to border on delusion, Breckenridge's voice and the ensuing glower that he cast upon Davis were soul piercing. "Sir, what few men I still command have mostly discarded their weapons, and the ones who remain under arms will not ride into a general engagement unless coerced." Rising above the diminutive temptation to opportunistically taunt the executive by bringing it to his attention that the paper army of five brigades that surrounded Abbeville were at the very best a rank-heavy light brigade of three thousand men, five generals, a secretary of war and a half-crazed commander in chief, Breckenridge countered, "The only cause for these men to ride on is not to continue this war or launch a guerilla movement that will cause an exponential amount of suffering to our people; no sir, the war is over." Staring directly into the burning eyes of the Magnolia State's greatest politician, the flea continued to gnaw away at the lion: "To provide you with your answer, the only reason that they ride on is to ensure your safety and to get you out of the country."[181]

The peculiar contortion of the president's face was a side effect of an internal conundrum that drove his heavily bruised psyche into a queer state that ranged between shock, dread, contempt and utter insecurity. Acknowledging Breckenridge's opinion, Davis then prodded Brigadier General Basil Duke for his assessment of the situation. Not wasting a single breath with the customary mincing of words that the cantankerous president had long grown to expect from intimidated subordinates, Duke succinctly summarized Breckenridge's opinions in unequivocal concurrence. After completing his own assessment of the military situation that confronted the isolated band, the general concluded with the unnerving avowal that, should the group elect to continue the war, it would be a damnable affront to their men, which no justification could ever validate.[182]

Thanking his junior brigadier general and prodding the next senior-most officer to sport the wreath-encircled triple stars, Davis's disappointment continued. Both Dibrell and Ferguson concurred with the previous two opinions. Ferguson, however, went on to add a gloomy sense of earnest to the meeting by pointing out to his livid superior that the few thousand armed men who were still loyal to the Confederacy could not possibly break through the ensnarement that was rapidly developing around their party. The only rational conclusion, according to Ferguson, was to divide the party in multiple directions and send the president off with a small band of dedicated cavalry. At that point, it became all too clear to the renegade politician that in the minds of his surviving commanders, the war was indeed over.[183]

Following Ferguson's earth-shattering statement, Vaughn concurred with the plan and began to outline a strategy for the division of the remaining troops before Davis quieted him. Turning to his old reliable acquaintances, Generals Breckenridge and Bragg, and his chief of staff, Colonel William Preston Johnston, Davis's desperate stares for approval were met with diverted eyes and wringing hands. The president was truly alone in his opinion that the disagreeable course of the war was only an intermission, and the realization of his solitude washed over him in a frigid tide. Brooding quietly for over a dozen minutes, the room was saturated in tension as every ill emotion imaginable molded the face of the contemplator.[184]

Finally exploding out of his chair and turning from the table without excusing himself, it was clear that the conversation was not over, a disturbing prospect that the useless bloodshed would continue. In a foreboding sign of what was to come, as the exhausted president attempted to vacate the room, the weary traveler wavered in mid-stride. The tumbling executive would have collapsed right before the eyes of his senior officers had it not been for the nimble feet of General Breckenridge, who sprung up and grabbed the waving arm of the executive.[185]

With Davis vacating the room for the relaxing comforts of a sofa in the adjoining lounge, the remaining inhabitants of the dining room began to map out details for the unapproved fracturing that would hopefully save their impotent commander's neck. It was there, as the mid-afternoon sun cast its long shadows across the eastern side of the dining room in Abbeville's Burt Mansion, that Davis lost any remaining threads of power still clutched between his fingers. No longer was he the commander in chief of one of the greatest armies that had ever roamed the earth. Instead, the sickly man was a valuable package that the generals had sworn to keep out of the vindictive hands of their triumphant adversary.[186]

The heartbreaking scene that was the final war council of the Confederacy, held late in the afternoon of May 2, 1865, in the sleepy backwater of Abbeville, South Carolina, was a full month in the making. The midnight exodus of Jefferson Davis and a volunteer guard under Secretary of War General John C. Breckenridge from Abbeville on May 3 was an earth-shattering reverse from the situation that the politician had found himself in at the beginning of April. As the main body of the cavalry guard continued into Georgia under General Duke, the various cabinet secretaries—who were not invited to the final function of the Confederate government—would escape with

Wearing more hats than any other member of the Confederate high command, John Cabell Breckenridge had a remarkable political and military career that spanned allegiance to both nations. While he sought to preserve the freedom of the renegade president, in the end, Breckenridge could only save his own neck by becoming one of the few members of the Confederate inner circle to safely make it out of the South. *Courtesy of the Library of Congress.*

While at the apex of his political career when the war began, Davis struggled in vain to circumvent a widely forecasted prognosis for the Confederacy: death by theory. *Courtesy of the Library of Congress.*

the treasury. With the slender war chest of the Confederacy crossing into Georgia, driven by the unrealistic goal of transporting it to Cuba in order to finance a government in exile, Davis could not help but look back to the morning of April 2 and the final hours before his fragile house of cards came crashing down.[187]

It was just a few moments before eleven o'clock in the morning, and the president was walking with a small entourage from the executive mansion to his regular Sunday morning haunt: St. Paul's Episcopal Church. At that moment, the postmaster general of the Confederacy, John Reagan, rode up to the small party and handed Davis a telegraph. The memo, which had been hastily scribbled by the arthritic hand of Robert E. Lee while the aging general watched Union skirmishers from the Sixth Corps advance across all points of his front, informed the commander in chief that the Army of Northern Virginia's lines were pierced in at least a half dozen places, and his defenses were untenable. Coolly reading the telegram and penning a response on the reverse side, Davis continued his gentle stroll to morning services without even a hint of duress.[188]

The response that Davis sent to his pressed army was as foolhardy as the president was pigheaded. Tragically for Lee's exhausted enlisted men, the order smacked of the same dreamy belief in the invincibility of Confederate forces that had plagued Davis's tenure in the nation's highest office. In his eyes it was impractical to abandon the position because no forewarning had been given of the collapse, and the government's valuables had not yet been crated. Following Lee's receipt of the message, this normally coolheaded sage became infuriated at the final demonstration of insulation from the suffering of his men by an ignorant political arena in Richmond. Disavowing the president's concern, Lee wired Davis that Petersburg and Richmond would be abandoned by nightfall in an effort to save his army and the war effort.[189]

Knowing what ills the rising sun would bring, the late evening evacuation was not an easy undertaking. In one of the saddest days of the Mississippian's life, Davis boarded the cabinet train bound for Danville with the intention of establishing a temporary capital of the Confederacy. As the cars labeled by department pulled away from the depot, everyone but Davis suspected that the Southern administration would not return to its home and that this would be the last time that the third national would fly atop the old city. The exile in Danville lasted until April 10, when the earth-shattering news that Lee had surrendered his army the day before arrived at the president's residence.[190]

Acknowledging that the situation in Virginia was temporarily out of its hands, the government boarded trains in preparation for a move into North Carolina. Later in the afternoon, now secretary of war John C. Breckenridge, Joseph E. Johnston, Pierre Gustave Toutant Beauregard and Jefferson Davis met with the intention of devising a plan to review the Confederate war effort. While the generals urged Davis to acknowledge that the war was lost and that preparations for his flight be made, the stubborn president refused and ordered Johnston to succeed in an action where Lee had failed: continued resistance. Responding to a man that he had never truly liked, Johnston quipped that he was not in the Thermopylae business and made it clear that his intention was to seek the most favorable terms possible with General Sherman.[191]

Following his meeting with the remaining theater commanders, Davis's fortune slowly dwindled. Arriving in Greensboro by rail late on the night of the tenth, Davis held out in central North Carolina for five days in an attempt to present the aesthetic of normalcy. Then, on the fifteenth, reality

Seemingly fighting an uphill battle for the majority of the war in every major theater of operation, Pierre Gustave Toutant Beauregard's long battle came to an end alongside Johnston near Durham, North Carolina. *Courtesy of the Library of Congress.*

came crashing down on the withered soul. Sending his wife and children on a trek to the Deep South by carriage under the careful auspices of his personal secretary, Burton Harrison, Davis departed the town on horseback in the direction of Charlotte because the connecting rails had been rendered useless by Stoneman's efforts.[192]

On April 18, Davis arrived in Charlotte. Renewed in grit and defiance, he began to diligently organize the core of what he hoped would later serve as the foundation of a continued resistance. Five brigades of cavalry, barely surpassing three thousand men at roll call, served as his escort into South Carolina. On the afternoon of the twenty-sixth, the unpleasant situation disintegrated into anarchy as Johnston surrendered the last major Confederate army east of the Appalachian Mountains to Sherman.[193]

It was the hope of both rival western commanders that the common-sense peace the pair handcrafted would graciously allow the South enough time to reorganize itself before the spoils of war were divvied up by the ferocity of the kangaroo government in Washington. An issue of particular importance to the Confederate commander was the flight of Jefferson Davis, which had a glimmer of hope due to Sherman's apathy toward capturing the renegade president. The counterproductive actions taken by Sherman, which included inadvertently ordering the remnants of Stoneman's force out of Davis's route, spun Secretary of War Edward Stanton into a tirade. Stanton, irate at the possibility that his highest-ranking officer in the Tar Heel State was engaged in sabotage, dispatched Ulysses S. Grant to North Carolina in an effort to ensure that the fiery Ohioan was not derelict in his orders to bring the rebellion to a close. Upon learning of the developments, Davis abandoned North Carolina for its southern counterpart with his large entourage, arriving in Fort Mill late on the evening of the twenty-seventh.[194]

The next morning, at the home of Colonel William Elliott White, the last cabinet meeting of the Confederacy's executive branch was called to order. The meeting reeked of impending disaster as many options were laid on the table, choices that ranged from establishing a government in exile to inaugurating an expansive guerrilla war in every Southern state. The most practical option considering the circumstance—strategic exile—was refused by Davis. Even though his diplomatic actions could have been supported by the large chest of treasure accompanying him on his flight, the total sum was nowhere near the hefty fortune reported by Northern newspapers and could in no way sustain an active army in the field.[195]

After the meeting's adjournment, the president proceeded in a carriage toward Yorktown. Making slow progress on the twenty-eighth, Davis was made aware that his family was resting safely in Abbeville—much to his elation and relief. Applying the strap to his team on the twenty-ninth, Davis made rapid progress into the upstate by passing through both Unionville and Cross Keys. Slicing through the eastern extremes of the upstate, Davis arrived in Abbeville mid-morning on May 2 after a few days of hard riding and visitation with local supporters.[196]

Understanding that time was of the essence, and that the sizeable entourage accompanying the president was rapidly transforming into a signal beacon for thousands of pursuers, the final war council of the Confederacy was held. It was at this juncture that the heartbreaking decision to dissolve his escort and abandon the war effort was made. To compound the hardship handed the fugitive in picturesque Abbeville, Davis grudgingly accepted the resignation of Secretaries Stephen Mallory and Judah P. Benjamin, two men who had served him faithfully through the course of the war. Early in the morning of May 3, the volunteer force under John C. Breckenridge departed with their high-value accompaniment and made for the river that dissects South Carolina and Georgia.[197]

One of only a handful of the Confederate high command who hailed from foreign soil, Stephen Mallory was one of the final figures who approved the dissolution of the Rebel government at Washington, Georgia, on May 5. *Courtesy of the Library of Congress.*

Holding the offices of attorney general, secretary of war and secretary of state, Judah Philip Benjamin was the jack-of-all-trades in the Confederate regime and one of the few Confederate politicians to remain with Davis until the disintegration of the skeleton government. *Courtesy of the Library of Congress.*

Crossing the Savannah River by mid-morning, the Confederate figurehead advanced on to Washington, Georgia, where his family arrived to be by his side. On the morning of the fourth, the renegade first family and a small cavalcade of armed supporters departed Washington, inaugurating the final leg of their flight—a quest for the safety of an isolated Florida port and freedom in Cuba. It was at that point that the race turned desperate. Knowing full well that there were no fewer than two independent cavalry divisions trying to cut short his exodus, Davis attempted to employ every trick his genius mind could muster to avoid capture. While Major General James Wilson's command was hoping to dissect the fugitive's path and capture him before he crossed the Florida border, Palmer's three brigades desperately bit through the dust to hound the president's trail.[198]

No sooner had the president departed than the well-honed plan drafted in Abbeville fell apart. The bulk of the command, which tentatively abided the degenerative leadership of Duke, Dibrell and Vaughn, crossed the Savannah River and immediately mutinied in order to seek terms with the raiders under Palmer. Having isolated themselves from the only objective

Seen here in his twilight years, George Gibbs Dibrell aided in negotiating terms for his exhausted and mutinous cavalrymen outside Washington, Georgia. *Courtesy of the Library of Congress.*

Although spending the majority of his wartime career in the background, East Tennessean John Crawford Vaughn increasingly grew in importance as the muster roll of Confederates depleted.

that kept them in the saddle, the remaining troopers under arms cast their lethal instruments to the ground and demanded that their commanders seek terms with their pursuers.

The darkest hour of the dying Confederacy had arrived as, whether through choice or condition, the entire band dissolved. John C. Breckenridge, while following a parallel road to mask the true location of the prized fugitive, was distraught to discover that he had lost contact with Davis around mid-afternoon. At that point, the most versatile Kentuckian in the entire country took it upon himself to send the treasury off with Judge John H. Reagan in an attempt to conceal it. While the president continued his flight, he was fatally unaware of the fact that two of the three fail-safes that covered his retreat had folded within a day of their organization.[199]

Perturbed and exhausted, the main body of his cavalry escort simply ceased to exist. The core component of the resistance that Davis had fantasized about personally leading to a resurrection of the Southern nation disbanded slightly southwest of Washington, Georgia. Well aware that the loyally disenchanted men had gone many months without pay, the final specie of the Confederate treasury was divided up and divvied out to its true owners. According to the overseer of the allocation, Brigadier General Duke, the silver coinage of the Confederate treasury was counted and then divided equally amongst the remaining officers and enlisted men who had bivouacked through morning roll call. Following the allotment

Understanding that the situation for the Confederacy was dire and ultimately impossible should his task fail, John H. Regan departed Davis's company in hopes of reaching sanctuary with the Confederate treasury. *Courtesy of the Library of Congress.*

of the treasure, the officers of the band were polled. Keenly aware of the hopelessness of their situation, coupled with the clutter of carbines strewn across the camp, the electors decided to make peace with their pursuers—or at least that's how it appeared on the surface.[200]

At approximately the same time Palmer's division completed its crossing of the Savannah River slightly upstream. Its southerly course brought it within earshot of the Confederate camp in just a matter of hours. While Palmer was inundated with the task of observing the questionable movements of the Second and Third Brigades, direct command of the First Brigade passed into the hands of Colonel Charles M. Betts. The virgin brigade commander, along with Palmer, went into camp just south of the Savannah River slightly past midnight on the morning of May 4. As their pickets penetrated the thick Georgia brush, wayward Confederate deserters poured out of the woodwork.[201]

As the camp filled with the sunken faces of Confederate scarecrows, the resolve of their foe became all too clear. In no time, extracted less through persuasion than reward, information was espoused regarding the Confederate situation. The news that filled the integrator's ears was delightful. The president of the Confederacy was isolated with a solitary band under General Breckenridge, and the bulk of that force was only a few miles down the road spoiling for peace.[202]

With reports flowing in from numerous sources that Davis and his entourage were just eighteen miles away at Washington, the First Brigade sprung into action. Driving their mounts faster than any pace the poor beasts had undertaken before, the tall needle pines passed by their peripherals like enormous blades of grass. On point, the Thirteenth Tennessee Cavalry pushed deeper into Georgia than any element of the raid had yet ventured, until its advance guard was halted. The abrupt stop was not the result of gunfire but instead the surprise of a half-limp white flag held by one of the pickets of Colonel Breckenridge's command.[203]

No sooner had contact been made than a peculiar sight surfaced. There, in the early morning mist of a tick-infested picket post, stood a senior officer. In a poignant example of poetic justice, the officer in question was the outspoken Colonel Breckenridge. The combative officer, who had recently shattered the aspirations of his commander in chief, posted himself at the extreme rear in anticipation of suffering the humble task of delivering the news of capitulation to the pursuing Federal troopers.[204]

Under a flag of truce, Breckenridge approached the commanding sergeant of the advance guard and informed him that the skeletal brigades that rested farther down the road wished to come to terms with Stoneman. Informed that the New Yorker was long absent from his command, Breckenridge inquired as to the identity of the commanding officer and whether the man in question could be contacted as soon as possible. Informed that a Pennsylvanian was the director of the pursuers, Breckenridge told the advance guard that he wished to inaugurate a dialogue with its superiors. The startled pickets were taken aback by the turn of fortune; after gathering their senses, a messenger was sent to the rear to inform Betts of the developments.[205]

Once Betts was made aware that a parlay was inaugurated just a mile down the road, the fresh brigade commander stalled. Finally, after a few moments of pondering, he ordered a messenger to inform Palmer of the fortunate developments. After the rider conferred with Palmer, word reached Betts that the parley was to be held and that the same terms that were common to both Lee's and Johnston's command were to be offered the secluded brigades.

Following the messenger's return, Betts commenced to express the wishes of his superior to a nervous Confederate counterpart. With Palmer's request obliged, Breckenridge paused as he processed the terms in his mind. After an uncomfortable silence, he pressed the Union commander for a generous amount of time in which to consider the provisos and present them for approval to his subordinates. To the everlasting regret of the First Brigade, the request was honored.[206]

Unbeknownst to Betts or Palmer, the request was nothing more than a well-calculated ruse designed to afford the renegade president enough of a head start to evade his pursuers. While the men of the three brigades had elected to succumb to the looming Union tide, they did so with a rancor that twisted the stomachs of the saddle-sore Federal troopers. The peace negations, which lasted the entirety of the night, gave Davis a twelve-hour advantage against his pursuers. Indeed, the actions of the contemplative colonel afforded his ideological adversary a few extra sunsets as the commander of a deceased nation.[207]

Early the following morning, May 5, Palmer's command continued its pursuit. After paroling the Confederate bait, the First Brigade continued toward Athens, still oblivious to the fact that they had been had by the Confederate schemers. About noon, the First Brigade arrived at the

According to tradition, and a few eyewitness accounts, Jefferson Davis took it upon himself to lead his ever-dwindling following once it crossed the Savannah River. *Courtesy of the Library of Congress.*

predetermined rendezvous point of Athens, Georgia. Resting their mounts on the greenery of the defunct university, Palmer established a headquarters in the old Georgia town and opened his ears to accounts of misdeeds conducted by his other two brigades.[208]

The city, one of the most beautiful in Georgia, was afforded total impunity under the command of Palmer. There are no written accounts of looting, as the town was swarming with enough paroled Confederate and enlisted men that if the opportunity had arisen, an effective resistance could have been mounted. It was at Athens that the men of the First Brigade came to the rational conclusion that the war was over, and now they were merely Federal agents in pursuit of a renegade fugitive. It was also at the university town that Palmer came to the realization that the other two brigades of his command had devolved into a state of anarchy and were no longer useful to the cause of Union. Wiring to his ultimate superiors in Tennessee, Palmer requested that Brown's and Miller's Brigades be withdrawn from the expedition at once, lest they continue their horrific actions against the civilians of the region.[209]

Although the railroad lines throughout North and South Carolina had been severed in a plethora of locations due to recent Federal activity, the track that coursed through Georgia had been relatively repaired in the aftermath of Sherman's conquest of the state. Knowing that the lines

The chapel at the University of Georgia not only was left idle by the middle years of the war but was also done disservice by its use as a barracks during the brief Federal occupation of Athens, Georgia. *Courtesy of the Library of Congress.*

connecting Athens with Augusta and Atlanta were in operation, Palmer dispatched small detachments down these tracks in hopes of intercepting a train carrying Davis. While it was widely believed that Davis would naively arrive in Federal-occupied Athens by rail at any hour, the long-expected interception of the fugitive was not to be. Unfortunately for Palmer's designs, the renegade president had elected to stick to the dirt roads in an attempt to remain incognito.[210]

Dispatching two hundred men to Madison, Georgia, under First Lieutenant John F. Conway, the troopers intercepted a train full of Confederate parolees who inhabited a series of cars that the president was rumored to be on. Knowing that Davis could be seated on any number of trains that might steam down the line, the detachment destroyed a large section of the track and set up camp along the Oconee River. Having established headquarters in Athens and organized a posse from his only loyal brigade, Palmer wired General Wilson's headquarters in Macon. Informing his counterpart that the raiders had most likely forced Davis to adopt a route that took him closer to the region Wilson's men were patrolling, the two opened a dialogue in an effort to apprehend the wily fugitive.[211]

While the general was gnawing away at the head start Davis had accumulated over Palmer, some of the troopers had uncovered an unexpected laurel that was a fair consolation for their failure to apprehend the $100,000 man in South Carolina. On May 6, along the shady banks of the slow-flowing Appalachee River, a scouting detachment of the Fifteenth Pennsylvania, under Willis Reffry, happened upon a series of Confederate mule skinners resting their teams. The members of the lightly defended wagon train, which consisted of seven old Conestoga wagons, instantly knew that they were outgunned and surrendered without any resistance. The unimposing train, after further exploration revealed its nature, happened to carry the remainder of the mythical Confederate treasury that had departed Richmond on April 2.[212]

Disbelieving what their eyes were telling them, the men of the Fifteenth Pennsylvania exercised extraordinary restraint in their seizure of the transitive fortune. Seven wagons, drug through the muddy spring roads of northeastern Georgia by twenty-three draft horses of French Norman stock, were loaded with a horde that stressed the exhausted axels of the inconspicuous vehicles. With wide eyes befalling the cargo, Reffry's men instantly knew that their prize was one of the greatest captures of currency that the war had witnessed. The remainder of the Confederate war chest did in fact include the coveted cache of gold that every man in the Union longed to place his hands on. Although 188,500 gold dollars were divided among four iron-locked chests, the stash was noticeably lighter than the multiple millions of dollars in bullion that the Northern newspapers had touted.[213]

In addition to gold, the wagon trains held a plethora of worthless script masquerading as legal tenure. In all, $645,000 in state currency and bonds was lovingly bundled in the wagons, accompanied by $4,265,500 of severely depreciated Confederate currency. In addition to the worthless scraps of paper, $480,000 in securities from the Central Railroad and Banking Company of Georgia was stacked beside $460,500 in notes from the Bank of Macon. Even after the faithful Confederate troopers were paid their just rewards, $68,000 in silver coinage was uncovered in the wagons.[214]

The wealth of the wagons was not relegated to government holdings alone. Piled high in countless steamer trunks and carpet bags were over $2,000,000 worth of personal belongings, all of which had been added to the trove by the inhabitants of the upstate of South Carolina and northeastern Georgia for safekeeping. Rummaging through the massive quantities of silver and gold trinkets, the men of the Fifteenth Pennsylvania once again demonstrated uncanny discipline in ensuring that the names of the owners of the additional baggage were well documented. In addition to the civilian articles, the personal belongings of Generals Pierre Beauregard and Gideon J. Pillow were bundled within the rails of the wagons.[215]

Staring a life of luxury in the face, which could have been easily assumed through selective thievery, the men of the Fifteenth Pennsylvania took the high road. Under the leadership of a sergeant who had been detailed ten trustworthy followers, the wagons were returned to Athens without the loss of a single article of property or treasure. Palmer remembered the arrival of the wagons for the remainder of his life and was later noted as saying that he was more proud of the treasure-laden wagons' safe return to Athens than any other event or battle of his wartime experience. After the arrival of the treasure in Athens, it was dispatched to Augusta with the intention that the horde be stored in the Federal arsenal under the care of General Apton. There it remained untouched until the personal property could be returned to its rightful owners—one of the early efforts of reconciliation in the Southeast.[216]

On May 7, the cold trail of Davis once again began to steam. Throughout the brigade, word came from various scout details that the renegade Mississippian and the impotent Braxton Bragg were reported to have been spotted in Fair Play, Georgia, at approximately three o'clock that very morning. By mid-afternoon, Palmer and his command had departed Athens in hopes of finally cornering the fugitive party. Arriving at the crossroads about ten o'clock that night, the rumors were validated, and a satisfied Palmer afforded his men three hours of sleep in hopes of capturing the slow-moving Davis with refreshed mounts the next morning. At one o'clock in the morning, the pursuit was resumed, and the command maintained a hellish pace until it finally broke at Covington in the neighborhood of six o'clock on the eighth. Following the establishment of a base camp, Palmer ordered the local population to feed his men and drew sufficient fodder for his horses from the local stables.[217]

In the middle of dinner, a report that made Palmer's heart jump into his throat crossed the table. The Twelfth Ohio, a cornerstone of the First Brigade, reported that it had cornered Davis's party near Conyers Station and that the renegade president was within grasp. The report, however, was premature. Instead of capturing the $100,000 human prize, the regiment had finally apprehended elusive Confederate cavalry commander Joseph Wheeler and a fourteen-man entourage. The general, who decades later donned the blue uniform that he had forsaken to fight the Spanish Empire in Cuba, was a

Captured while trying to make his way toward the Confederate resistance in Texas, Joseph Wheeler was a constant pariah of many Union officers, particularly George Stoneman. *Courtesy of the Library of Congress.*

constant pariah of the Union army throughout the course of the war. His later-life change in allegiance led an aging James Longstreet to remark at a Confederate reunion that he hoped death would take him before Wheeler so Longstreet could wait at the gates of hell on the off chance that he would have the satisfaction of seeing the expression on their comrade and devout secessionist Jubal Early's face when Wheeler arrived in a blue uniform.[218]

Having tormented the cavalry commanders of the Union for years, the cunning general was apprehended with forged parole papers in hand, attempting one last ruse by passing himself off as one Lieutenant Sharp. With a recognizable face, the general quickly owned up to his persona and mounted his most famous trophy—a fine painted pony that had once belonged to Union general Judson Kilpatrick, which Wheeler had stolen from him as the Union commander was surprised in camp wearing nothing but his underwear by the hard-riding Georgian—to peacefully follow his captors. Returning to Palmer's command, the general rode un-harassed, as the blue-clad troopers were in awe, finally coming face to face with a boogeyman that had haunted them for over three years.[219]

The war was immersed in contradictions for Alfred Iverson, seen here in his elderly years. Vilified for the possibly alcohol-induced slaughter of his own brigade of infantry on the first day of the Battle of Gettysburg and subsequently dismissed from duty, he was reborn as a cavalry commander in Georgia during the Atlanta Campaign. It was there that he took the highest-ranking prize of the entire war: Major General George Stoneman. *Courtesy of the Library of Congress.*

Later in the day, General Alfred Iverson was also apprehended by the Twelfth Ohio. In an episode of poetic justice that delighted Stoneman to no end, the two men who had cornered and captured the raid's father the previous summer—Iverson and Wheeler—were now in Federal custody. With the dawning of May 9, Braxton Bragg, one of Jefferson Davis's last true supporters in his flight, was apprehended by a party under Lieutenant Samuel Philips outside Irwin, Georgia. While Bragg contended that he was on his way to Macon for a peaceful

Detested by many of the troops that served under the authoritarian general, Braxton Bragg had the utmost confidence in Jefferson Davis—even until the very end of their secessionist efforts. *Courtesy of the Library of Congress.*

surrender to General Wilson, the general had most likely attempted a final fragmentation from the president's party. This final partition was undertaken in hopes of once again throwing the pursuers off the president's trail and securing his only friend in the world further comfort by riding ahead to recruit safe houses along his trek. As the general once described as an untrustworthy porcupine was taken into custody, the last vestiges of the Confederate high command ceased to exist. Davis was now truly alone.[220]

The loin-tingling satisfaction of the long-awaited meeting, a sensation over a month in the making, was not to be experienced by the troopers under Palmer on that fateful morning. While Davis later acknowledged that it was Palmer who had cut him off and retarded his adventure, troopers from the Fourth Michigan of Wilson's command had the honors of apprehending the most wanted man in the world. On the morning of May 10, Davis's party was stopped along a creek outside Irwin. The party, sound asleep due to exhaustion, was awakened from their tents by the sounds of sporadic unaimed gunfire.[221]

As Davis kissed Varina and took one of her shawls to conceal his face, the president lifted a pail and nonchalantly advanced toward the swamp in an effort to escape into the aquatic brambles while the troopers breeched the makeshift camp. Even though his guard claimed that they were wayfaring travelers in search of respite, the Michigan men were a little too keen to think that such a large collection of able-bodied men was anything but a security detail for the important man. Dissecting the camp, a cache of weapons was uncovered, and it became clear that the elusive prey had finally been

Left: Rivaling the ferocity of Stoneman's command throughout the final weeks of the war, the men under James Harrison Wilson were responsible for apprehending the fugitive president. *Courtesy of the Library of Congress.*

Below: At the bequest of his wife, Jefferson Davis donned a shawl as he attempted to slip away from his overrun camp. This allowed northern newspaper men and humorists the license to boast that the renegade president was apprehended wearing women's clothes. *Courtesy of the Library of Congress.*

cornered. Scanning the surrounding pasture, having not directly confronted the man of interest, two women were observed scampering off toward the tree line. After being ordered to halt, the duo continued unresponsive.[222]

Noticing the glint of spurs on one of the two women walking toward the swamp, a sixth sense came over the troopers—most notably Corporal George Munger. Overcome with the feeling that this was the long-awaited moment, a handful of troopers mounted and rode down the pair without orders. The pursuers leveled their carbines at the mysterious laborers, and the president unhinged his shawl.[223]

It takes no stretch of the imagination to understand that Davis was instantly recognized by the astonished troopers. As the most reviled member of the Southern Confederacy, Davis's likeness had graced broadsheets plastered on walls and illustrated in newspapers throughout the North. Truly, his distinctive features could be mistaken for none other. Allowing the shawl to drape its weight on his defeated shoulders, Davis owned up to his identity without incident. The unexpected circumstances surrounding his

For the next few decades, Davis was subjected to personal slander due to his leadership role in the Confederacy and the public's fascination with his unusual capture. *Courtesy of the Library of Congress.*

This illustration expresses the outrage and suspicions that many in the United States harbored following the cessation of hostilities and the assassination of Abraham Lincoln. *Courtesy of the Library of Congress.*

actual capture later gave Northern newspapers the liberal license to claim that the villain of the war had been apprehended in women's clothing.[224]

Denied the satisfaction of wearing the mantel of captors, the men under Palmer continued their fool's errand in earnest for five more days. On May 15, the troopers of the First Brigade were notified that the renegade president had been captured in southeast Georgia nearly a week earlier. The disappointment was bitter, yet the news brought comfort in knowing that the conflict was finally over. As word spread throughout the command, company after company launched a cheer of approval for the news.[225]

The glory wrought from the most important capture of the war was not to shine on Palmer. However, in a rare example of fraternalism between Union generals, credit due became credit earned. Later, Palmer wrote that Wilson had proclaimed that the capture was only the result of the raiders' efforts, as the Pennsylvanian had driven the game into the bag that Wilson's men held.

While the Northern public largely abhorred the supposed luxurious accommodations of Jefferson Davis, the image could not have been further from the truth. In reality, the renegade president was under continuous guard and spent the majority of his days in a claustrophobic cell. *Courtesy of the Library of Congress.*

Comforted by the fact that his men had captured the treasury and the four mini-brigades that had been escorting Davis, the participants of the raid had a fitting end to their monumental journey.[226]

As the command wheeled to the north and west, returning to their base of operations in Alabama and Tennessee, the long raid came to a sudden end. While the troopers would still be held in the service of the old flag well into the month of June, the war was essentially over for the three brigades. Setting course for the various regiments' respective destinations, the men began to reflect on what the previous six weeks had held for them: over two thousand miles of hard riding and the cementation of their commander's notorious reputation in the annals of the war. Having blocked Lee's last lines of escape, crippled the dying Confederacy through infrastructure destruction and—as George H. Thomas had also said—driven the presidential prey into the bag that Wilson held, the three brigades ended their wartime experience on a high note. This was a claim that many regiments of the Union army could not make, as the majority of the blue-clad soldiers spent their final weeks of the war waiting to be dismissed and lounging away in camp with their hardest labors behind them.

Epilogue

"We Are Suffering More from Our Own Raiders than We Possibly Could from Yankee Discipline"

An acrid aroma, descending from the loft and thickly blanketing the room like a cold January fog, was all the indication needed to bring every soul in the room to the same conclusion simultaneously: "Jesus Christ! Those bastards have touched the roof afire!" Diverting his attention from the porthole that he was manning, Wade cast a swift eye about the room. The panoramic survey filled his brain with images that were not encouraging. Locked in an instantaneous stare with over two dozen eyes that were steeped in the frantic horror indicative of their imminent demise, the faltering commander's only reassurance in the group's catastrophic plight came from the six or seven indifferent laborers who continued to saturate the surrounding hillside with repeating arms fire.

Diligently creeping along the wall that he was protecting with a half dozen other trapped rats, Wade was weary of the open portholes and the possibility of accidentally exposing himself to a marksman's ball; that was, until he took note of the growing number of perforations born of the onslaught—a collection of holes that not only allowed stirred dust from the cabin floor to dance in beams of morning sunlight but also permitted the occasional projectile to pass through the thick walls unobstructed. Standing fully erect, surrendering his well-being to chance, Wade began his inquiry in earnest. Indeed, if the young Michigander's suspicions were steeped in fact, the walls of Fort Hamby would soon be leveled from the top as well as the bottom.[227]

Taking time to scan what his vantage point provided of the loft, he came to the conclusion that it was impossible to ascertain the origins of the rapidly concentrating vapor without leaving the ground floor. Mounting the ladder that crested the loft, Wade made a slow and cautious ascent. The vigilant escalade was necessary to avoid naively exposing his crown to any brazen assaulters who may have entered through the cedar shingles in an effort to ambush his band from within their own sanctuary. After two consecutive bobs between the hemispheres of the house, the surrounded pack leader was confident that the dark and tiny loft was secure. Finding momentary relief in his solitude, Wade dismounted the ladder and pushed into the shroud.

Clambering blindly over sacks of provisions that resulted from weeks of pillage, the rogue frantically searched for the source of the mantle. Collapsing the full weight of his body against the far wall as his boots became entangled in an unseen feed sack, the location of the destructive censer was betrayed by its radiating heat. Feeling the warmth spread its fingers across the expanse of his body, nerve-shattering nausea began to set in. Overcoming his momentary trepidation to unearth the degree of the roof fire, Wade squinted his eyes and advanced through the bellowing smoke. Untangling the empty sack from around the heel of his right boot and waving it in an effort to fan inroads through the veil, a momentary furrow revealed a horror to his parched corneas that the deepest recesses of his imagination could not have conjured in their best efforts.

The malicious actions of the besiegers were beyond successful. In just a short time, the flames had essentially engulfed the cedar slats covering the roof, and the extent of the blaze was made clear as the rafters began to smolder. Backpedaling, the inquisitor made no effort to vainly extinguish the growing inferno. Resigned to the hopelessness of further resistance within the thick walls of the fortified building, the beleaguered chief remounted the ladder and scuttled to the ground floor, lost in a haze of contemplation.[228]

As he locked eyes with the powder-stained face of a sandy-haired madam, her gray saucers betrayed the suppressed question that was festering in her throat: "How bad is the fire?" Forcing a lump back into the confines of his esophagus, Wade stood in silent contemplation while the various contingencies scattered through his head. Taking a cursory glance around the room at the rapidly deteriorating situation, Wade let out a meek whisper that seemed to drown out the ear-shattering retorts of rifles that were echoing throughout the small room: "We got to get the hell out of here, and fast."

Drawing a deep sigh that choked his lungs with the infernal gas, the bearer of ill news continued, "If we open up heavily on the north side of the house, we can draw them around to the front." Continuing his thought in an almost incomprehensible mutter, Wade silently mouthed the conclusion: "And if they bite, we will make for the tree line to the south." With his musing complete, the cold sensation of a room full of eyes firmly affixed on him began to slither over his skin. Emboldened by the prospect that his life was at an end, the brown-haired Michigander shook loose of his fears and clarified his proposal.

"Look!" He snapped his head toward the cadre of men who were rapidly reloading the sleeves of their Spencers in a vain effort to maintain suppressing fire. "That roof is lit with fire, and there isn't a goddamn thing that anyone can do about it." The news, although unnerving, came as no surprise to the men, who were beginning to choke under the weight of the lethal haze. As his twitching, adrenaline-saturated hands broke open the stock magazine of his own rifle in an effort to replenish the weapon, Wade continued, "If we pour it on them in one direction, then those bastards will assume that we are going to make good our escape from that side of the house."[229]

Sliding a few rounds down the magazine, Wade's voice began to burgeon in confidence. "They will move along the ridge in an effort to flank us." Pausing temporarily to secure the final round in its proper place, he continued, "That's when we can break and run for the opposite ridgeline." Casting another malevolent eye around the room for any sign of approval, the expression predominately worn by his gang was fearful reluctance. Returning the spring-loaded tube to the stock, his eyes looked to the loft as he snapped the butt plate in place. "They have already torched the kitchen and the south side roof. It wouldn't be long till we are in a world of hurt."

"To hell with that!" The gruff voice of one of the oldest men in the room, a Confederate deserter who had reluctantly paired with Wade in late April, filled the momentary silence. With the stalwart confidence of one who had survived the folly of similar schemes more times than he cared to remember, the detractor continued, "There's a full company out there. If we burst out of here in any direction, they will cut us down like dogs." As the obvious was stated, a few of the men who found themselves falling deeper in the recesses of paralysis began to nod in agreement.

Placing his back to the north wall, Wade aptly positioned himself next to a porthole. Risking the consequences of a full glance, the brigand presented a silhouette to his adversaries just long enough to build a better understanding of the scenario without drawing direct fire. The flirting glimpse filled his eyes enough to make him aware that a disciplined skirmish line was drawn along the slope of the hill. Doubling down on his luck, Wade took another glance at the north slope, and it was evident that the formation was advancing rapidly.

"They are tightening the noose boys. What is it going to be?" The question, although simplistic, was dripping with fatal undertones. After a few inaudible stammers, the majority of the riflemen shifted to Wade's side of the room and took up their respective positions along the north wall. After taking one last glance through his porthole, the landscape was dissolved by a bright muzzle flash. Momentarily blinding, the wrathful vent was immediately preceded by a ball that carved the open air—clearly, the final assault was upon them. "Pin them down," was the only utterance that his shocked sense could produce.

The rapid saturation of lead had its desired effect, as the assault of the local militia fell back almost instantly. Seconds later, cries declaring that the inhabitants were attempting to flee the flames from the unlit northern side of Fort Hamby rose up across the surrounding skirmish line. "Empty out and make for the back door quickly!" The adrenaline-saturated words darted out of Wade's mouth as he frantically worked the firing mechanics of his Spencer. The rapid pops of .52-caliber rifles once again echoed through the room as the besieged captain cleared his magazine.

Dropping his hammer on the final rim-fire cartridge to slide into the chamber that morning, the bandit Moses turned to rush for the south wall in anticipation of readying the backdoor lock. As the clicks of dry fires began to resonate throughout the room, a herd of worried outlaws and prostitutes surged toward the back door. In an instant, Wade threw the lock and pulled the rope that opened the gnarled door. With frightened eyes adjusting to make sense of the mixture of smoke and sunlight bellowing from the doorway, the stampede of desperados commenced.[230]

The hollow thud of a high-velocity projectile entering and exiting a nearby body cavity was the first sign that the dash for the timber was to be a hellish ordeal. Paying no attention to which man had been the unfortunate recipient of the home guard's marksmanship, Wade scanned the horizon of his flanks in horror. While the instinct of self-preservation rose to prominence, it became obvious that his plan was not as concrete as he had originally imagined. Elements of the informal militia had taken to their mounts and were attempting to sever his band's only avenue of retreat, all the while subjecting the fleeing rabble to the precise rifle fire of their dismounted members.

Ignoring the heavy reverberation of nearing hooves and the cries for quarter by those who had already been cutoff, Wade stormed to the front of his dwindling band. Eyes affixed on the nearing brambles and ears tuned to the nerve-shattering hiss of inaccurate projectiles, the fleeing kingpin was one of the first to crest the tree line. As the fir, hardwood and woolly-head obstacles began to snap under sporadic fire, the young Michigander frantically grabbed at limbs as he pulled himself to the crest of the ridge and the liberation that waited on the other side. In a flash, he and many others of his band were out of sight, bare of their provisions and, most devastating of all for their three-week venture, devoid of the plunder that had been extracted from the ravished populace of Wilkes County.[231]

While the bandit leader known as Wade was fortunate enough to escape with upwards of eighteen of his motley crew, four of the band members were taken alive. The only souls to face justice for a nearly month-long crime spree that developed in the wake of the Stoneman Raid were former Confederate deserters and members of the raid who had lost all semblance of discipline. Swiftly tied to fence posts by the impromptu militia under the leadership of Colonel George Washington Sharpe, four outliers—Beck, Church, Lockwood and one man who refused to divulge his identity—met their demise. Staring out at the great beyond, the four men were shot unceremoniously in their heads as the Appalachian bordello-turned-stronghold, known by the local populations as Fort Hamby, burned to the ground.[232]

Successfully violent, the third attempt at razing Fort Hamby was the climax of a three-week reign of terror that descended on the inhabitants of the Yadkin River Valley in the wake of the Stoneman Raid. As with many regions of the South, the inhabitants of isolated enclaves found themselves at the mercy of renegade bands in the immediate months following the collapse of the Confederacy. While the bandits who rode with Wade and inhabited the home of an Appalachian madam by the surname of Hamby were ultimately scattered to the four winds, the momentary nightmare that they had induced on the ravished population only served to exacerbate the privations of a vanquished people. Their terrorism of the local inhabitants was stocked with sadistic deeds, including the slaying of a young child in front of its mother, the cold-blooded murder of a local reverend and the pilfering of what few valuable sundries remained in Wilkes County.[233]

The outlaw bands and chronic bushwhacking that continued to haunt the region were primarily facilitated by deserters from both armies. As discipline collapsed within the belligerent forces, those who chose to employ their martial skills for material gain did just that; it was rumored that Wade even subjected his men to drill once his band was formed. It should also be observed that the murders and robberies that continued into 1866 were the final salvos in a smoldering class conflict—a cultural test of strength that served as an ideological cornerstone for the war in western North Carolina. As with all conflicts, those who engaged in opportunistic banditry were either killed off, lost interest in their newfound avocation or eventually returned to the new societal folds created by the cessation of hostilities.[234]

While the cultural postwar turmoil that haunted the Appalachian region for the ensuing months began to intensify, the marauding force that had aided in laying the groundwork for such hardship was ending its Homeric journey several hundred miles away. Following substantiation of Jefferson Davis's capture by troopers under General Wilson, Palmer ordered the troopers under his command back to Athens for a reconsolidation. Upon their reunion, Palmer's concern over the undisciplined nature of Brown's and Miller's commands only deepened.

As Stoneman's order for an expedient return to their home base in Knoxville crossed the brevetted commander's desk, Palmer thought it best to keep his rogue elements under thumb. Short of removing his peers from command, the natural solution was to return the column en mass to the volunteer state. For undocumented reasons, however, the column arrived on the banks of the Tennessee River in piecemeal fashion, with a very relaxed chain of command and further plunders in their saddlebags to show for it.[235]

The wide waters of the Tennessee River were the backdrop for the anticlimactic conclusion of the raid. Encamped on an unspecified neck of the river, Palmer and the Fifteenth Pennsylvania received signals from a Union gunboat that was patrolling the waterway with a message. After sending a dingy ashore, Palmer was presented with the long-anticipated orders from the raid's namesake: the war was over, and it was time to return home. The transcendental breath of accomplished relief was savored not a moment too soon. It was May 20 and just a few hours before the two-month anniversary of the inauguration of the raid.[236]

Straightforward and expected, the orders that Palmer received that day were a godsend. Taking the origins of the division's brigades into consideration, the command was dissected and spread across the volunteer state. Palmer was instructed to ride with his First Brigade to Nashville in preparation of debriefing Stoneman on the raid's later developments and to reinforce the cavalry presence in central Tennessee. The Second and Third Brigades were ordered to return immediately to their home base of Knoxville. There, discipline was to be restored and the units mustered out of service. While the men under Palmer's charge reported as quickly as their tired mounts and the worn condition of their equipment would allow, the other two brigades took their sweet time in returning to Knoxville, ultimately leaving some of the Southern-born companies in the field and in service well into November.[237]

In the ensuing months, the various regiments to which the raiders belonged disbanded. Most of the members, as is the nature of minor players in history, faded into obscurity, leaving their personal legacies at the mercy of genealogists and their memories embodied in the minds of future descendants who took interest in their small contributions to the Union war effort. Others rose to prominence in state and federal politics, as well as in the ranks of veterans' associations. As with most regimental structures during the war, those who held notable positions of command carried over their limelight into the postbellum civilian world. The principal players of the raid were no exception, although their postwar careers varied greatly.

Simon B. Brown, the turbulent commander of the Second Brigade, whose questionable laurels included both the sackings of Asheville and Anderson, received his decommission on June 11 at Lenoir, Tennessee. After his release from service, he returned to his native Michigan to pick up right were he left off—managing the affairs of his hotel in St. Clair and resuming his duties as county alderman. While seemingly a lackluster ending for a brigade commander, his life was happy and fulfilling until a tragic night in January 1873. For some undisclosed reason, but most likely the fault of a chimney fire, his City Hotel was reduced to a pile of smoldering ash—poetic justice some would argue.[238]

To complicate matters further, Brown had not had the foresight to insure his property for the full weight of its worth. His frugal shortsightedness was costly, as he never fully recovered from the loss. Living a modest life for the remainder of his days, Brown died after succumbing to a series of illnesses, most notably two adversaries of the mounted soldier: the bleeding piles and obstinate constipation. Simon B. Brown died on March 16, 1893, at the ripe old age of eighty-one. He was buried with full military honors and much reverence by locals ignorant of the full scope of harm he inflicted on families nearly one thousand miles away.[239]

Indicative of his role in local politics at the start of the conflict, John Kelly Miller returned to Carter County and made a larger name for himself throughout East Tennessee. Immediately after the war, Miller was married for the second time and founded a company devoted to the manufacturing of wagons. Finding a knack for business, he later expanded his enterprises to include a dry goods store, an iron furnace and the operation of a hotel in Johnson City. Following the passage of the Excise Tax in 1866 and the creation of the Internal Revenue Service, Miller secured an appointment as a special collector of taxes on home distillation. While little is known of his experiences in this venture, considering the culture of the region to which he had been assigned, his job was certainly troublesome.[240]

In 1879, Miller made his foray into state-level politics by securing a seat in the Tennessee state senate. Finding success in this endeavor, he later convinced his constituency to allow him the opportunity to serve a momentary stint in the United States House of Representatives. Having built his reputation as a fierce field commander, a starch opponent of the paternalist culture of the antebellum South and a New South booster, Miller died quietly on June 10, 1903, at his home in Carter County.[241]

If his absence from the command following the truce negotiated along the Asheville Highway to attend the formation of the postbellum government in Tennessee was any indication of what the ensuing decades held for Alvan Cullem Gillem, then some of his later governmental missteps could easily be dismissed as overzealous ambition. Gillem sat in the Tennessee legislature for its first session of elected representatives after the war. But during the heart of his term, the politician was solicited with an appointment as a colonel in the regular army on July 28, 1866, and given oversight of the army occupation of Arkansas and Mississippi. However, much like other wartime commanders who were deemed too lenient on the vanquished for the exploding influence of Radical Republicans, he was soon replaced by one of General Grant's cronies and sent to a small outpost in California.[242]

It was there that military disaster and disgrace found him yet again. Commanding local forces during a conflict with the Modoc Nation, Gillem's men were subject to repeated ambush, and in one instance, nearly an entire column was wiped out. Disappointed with his performance, Colonel Gillem was relieved of duty on May 2, 1873, and sent back to Tennessee. It was there, in Nashville, that a relatively healthy Gillem succumbed to a fever in 1875.[243]

William Jackson Palmer, the warhorse of the entire raid, excelled in the postwar civilian world. Picking right up where he left off, Palmer ventured west to engage in railroad development. After serving as the Pennsylvania Railroad's point of contact along the Rocky Mountains, Palmer left their employment and founded his own railroad speculation venture in Colorado. By 1871, his business had proved so profitable that he established permanent residence in a town that he co-founded, Colorado Springs, and completed a mammoth mountain home, which he would inhabit for the remainder of his life.[244]

The war also had a rare way of following Palmer into his later life. As his civilian life was drawing to a close, experiences from long ago stormed headlong into the present. On February 24, 1894, Palmer was awarded the Congressional Medal of Honor for a notable episode of heroism that he undertook in the winter of 1865. Although not an episode of the raid, Palmer was given recognition for a charge he led on January 14 near Red Hill, Alabama. The charge, which enveloped and broke a Confederate defensive position, netted results of a captured fieldpiece and one hundred prisoners. Almost as miraculous, not a single one of Palmer's two hundred men were even so much as superficially wounded.[245]

Actively engaged in veterans' affairs, Palmer maintained continuous correspondence with his wartime subordinates in Pennsylvania. In late 1906, the old man was permanently paralyzed, suffering a spinal injury after being thrown from a horse. Bound to a wheelchair for the remainder of his life and confined to his mansion, Palmer's connections with the veterans of his former regiment became the catalyst for a fitting swan song in 1907, when the annual reunion of the Fifteenth Pennsylvania was held at Palmer's home in Colorado Springs. Never truly recovering from his late-life injury, Palmer died on March 13, 1909, at his home.[246]

It is no understatement to claim that the raid salvaged George Stoneman's military career. Prior to the successful completion of the operation, Stoneman was all but drummed out of service after being subjected to a multitude of tactical and strategic failures. However, with the triumphant arrival of the Fifteenth Pennsylvania at Nashville, Stoneman could now lay claim to the successful and independent cavalry operation that he had long theorized as possible.

After the immediate cessation of hostilities, Stoneman accepted a position as military commander of the Department of Tennessee. Much like his early efforts at the helm of smaller commands, Stoneman faltered under the face of unexpected pressure when a series of race riots rocked the city of Memphis from May 1 to May 3, 1866. As former Confederates hunted down black solders wholesale, Stoneman was remiss in his attempt to restore order, taking two full days to declare martial law. The end result was yet another inglorious mark on his service record and a dismissal from duty.[247]

Following the fiasco, Stoneman was removed from Memphis and transferred to oversee the military affairs in Petersburg, Virginia, in early December. It was there that Congress investigated him for the events of that spring. Although the legislative pariahs came to the conclusion that the general had done no wrong, Stoneman was not long for the military world.[248]

In September 1866, he was mustered out of volunteer service and commissioned as a lieutenant colonel in the regular service. Shortly afterward, George Stoneman was transferred to the West and spent the remainder of his service career performing poorly against various Indian uprisings in Arizona territory. By 1871, the army had had its fill of Stoneman's chronic lackluster performance and permanently relieved him of command that May.[249]

After his dismissal from the army, Stoneman sought a separation from the East and all the sore memories that it represented for him. Relocating to the same community in California that had captured his imagination during his prewar service, Stoneman made a modest home for himself. It was in the rolling hills of San Gabriel that his life finally began to make sense and opportunities started to present themselves. Since trained professionals were in short supply in California, Stoneman easily secured an appointment as state railroad commissioner—the first steppingstone in his short stint in politics.[250]

Having successfully completed his first foray into state office, Stoneman made a successful bid for governor in 1882. Although it was an office easily secured on his war record, he was only able to retain the gubernatorial mandate for a single term. Embroiled in conflict with his political banner, the Democratic Party, Stoneman was refused the nomination at the state convention during the next election cycle.[251]

Following his second return to civilian life, Stoneman's remaining time on earth was fraught with hardship and tragedy. Shortly after leaving office, Stoneman's home burned to the ground, most likely put to the torch by an arsonist. Without any insurance and only minimal savings, Stoneman was left essentially destitute.[252]

Returning to New York after tapping out his luck on the Pacific Coast, the old soldier quickly began to decline in health. Taken to his bed with a variety of illnesses, George Stoneman began to waste away. Then, on September 5, 1894, the raid's namesake died of a stroke in Buffalo, New York. In a tragic honorarium to his melancholic life, Stoneman was interred in a plot separate from his immediate family, who had chosen to relocate following his death, finally leaving him to fade into isolated obscurity in the company of distant relatives.[253]

The success of the raid is truly in the eye of the beholder. While it can be successfully argued that the raid was a strategic failure and only had a trivial impact on the outcome of the war—even General Grant went so far as to comment that the raid accomplished nothing but organized vandalism—it is undeniable that the raiders were diligent in their assigned labors. With dozens of bridges and trestles put to the torch, miles of railway track uprooted and mutilated, countless provisions incinerated and the final military stores of the dying Confederacy destroyed, the raid had a profound impact on the infrastructure of the Army of Northern Virginia and the Army of Tennessee.

Many of the regions that had succumbed to the raid were indeed handed a defeat that they might have otherwise escaped had the prowling armies come to terms without traversing their soil. With nary a suitable mount left in the tracks of the raiders, and the majority of fodder confiscated, the first agricultural season following the raid proved difficult for the locals—if not resulting in outright famine for some. Aside from the impact on the rural communities of the Appalachian rim, the urban centers of Salisbury, Asheville and Anderson were subjected to unnecessary hardships. With the exception of Salisbury, whose destruction of an infamous prison and rich stores of provisions aided in the collapse of further Confederate resistance, the actions taken by the raiders toward the urban inhabitants of the region benefited the Union war effort in no way whatsoever.

In smaller communities, the destruction of storehouses and factories may have impeded the possibility of an emerging guerrilla movement; however, this undertaking greatly hampered the postwar economic recovery. Although destructive in nature, the raid was not without its moments of charity. The cultural castoffs of the region, the Appalachian Unionists and recently emancipated blacks, were beneficiaries of circumstantial benevolence at the hands of the raiders. With countless records and traditions of their willingness to allow camp followers to cherry-pick the storehouses before the cache's incineration, the raiders took the first practical step at establishing the material well-being of those who had lived along the fringes of society during the antebellum period.

While the structural consequences of the raid were felt instantly, the cultural ones have lived on in the oral narratives and collective memory of the region long after the expiration of the raid's participants and victims. Well beyond highway landscapes dotted with iron historical markers and a one-line nod by Canadian musicians, the raid haunted the minds of the local populace. Even into the modern day, genealogists and local traditionalists throughout the region can recite the personal experiences of victims who died generations ago as if they were recent memory. Furthermore, many of the participants of the raid and their Southern origins have aided in the development of the image of the mountain loyalists during the conflict.

When all is said and done, the raid was merely a curiosity that paled in comparison to the epic battles of the war. In spite of being relegated to a footnote, the two-month odyssey became a respectable annotation. While voluminous libraries have been devoted to the large battles that ebbed and flowed for four hellish years, very few events from the most turbulent decade of our history have captured the imagination and memory of a civilian population more than the raid. In the end, much like the efforts of Sherman in Georgia and the Carolinas, the martial accomplishments of the Stoneman Raid will never be able to truly separate themselves from the cultural imprint that was left on the Appalachian rim.

Notes

Introduction

1. Van Noppen, *Stoneman's Raid*, 98.
2. Ibid. The following story is a narration of events surrounding the efforts of Generals Basil W. Duke and John Crawford Vaughn to shadow the column's advance toward Lincolnton, North Carolina. While many similar incidents occurred, the activities described in the following pages are the result of a narrative license taken with circumstantial evidence.
3. Throughout the closing days of the war, Southern civilians anxiously dreaded the arrival of not only Federal raiders but also rogue elements of the army that was supposed to be protecting them.
4. Van Noppen, *Stoneman's Raid*, 79.
5. *Landmark*, December 1, 1887; Van Noppen, *Stoneman's Raid*, 71.
6. For a contemporary account of the early weeks of the raid, see the preceding volume, *The Stoneman's Raid Begins: Leave Nothing for the Rebellion to Stand Upon.*
7. Bradshaw, "Stoneman's Raid"; *War of Rebellion*, series I, vol. 49, Part I, 324, 333–334; Fordney, *George Stoneman*, 114; Van Noppen, *Stoneman's Raid*, 67.
8. Kirk, *Fifteenth Pennsylvania*, 505; Trowbridge, "Stoneman Raid of 1865," 5; Starr, *Union Cavalry*, vol. 3, 452; Fordney, *George Stoneman*, 107, 117; Van Noppen, *Stoneman's Raid*, 71–72; *Landmark*, December 1, 1887; *War of Rebellion*, series I, vol. 49, part I, 663.
9. Andres, *History of St. Clair County*, 670; *Detroit Evening News*, "A Brave Man—Some Anecdotes of the Late General S.B. Brown," March 18,

1893; Keys, "Federal Pillage of Anderson," 84; *Knoxville Whig*, March 15, 1865; Civil War Centennial Commission of Tennessee, *Tennesseans in the Civil War*, vol. 1, 351–52; Scott and Angel, *History of the Thirteenth Tennessee*, 21–22, 112–13, 117, 138, 227, 255, 260, 263–64; Graf and Haskins, *Papers of Andrew Johnson*, vol. 7, 540–42; Black, *Cavalry Raids*, 185–86; *War of Rebellion*, series I, vol. 49, part I, 616.

10. *War of Rebellion*, series I, vol. 49, part I, 647; Kirk, *Fifteenth Pennsylvania*, 695; Van Noppen, *Stoneman's Raid*, 1–2.
11. Keys, "Federal Pillage of Anderson," 80–86.

CHAPTER 1

12. Van Noppen, *Stoneman's Raid*, 79–80.
13. Ibid., 80.
14. Ibid.
15. Ibid.
16. Ibid., 81–82.
17. Ibid., 80.
18. Ibid., 80–81.
19. Ibid., 81.
20. Ibid.
21. Ibid.
22. Ibid.
23. Barrett, *Civil War in North Carolina*, 363; *War of Rebellion*, series I, vol. 49, part I, 335; Van Noppen, *Stoneman's Raid*, 82; Black, *Cavalry Raids*, 190.
24. *War of Rebellion*, series I, vol. 49, part I, 335; Black, *Cavalry Raids*, 190; Barrett, *Civil War in North Carolina*, 363.
25. *War of Rebellion*, series I, vol. 49, part I, 335; Kirk, *Fifteenth Pennsylvania*, 507; Van Noppen, *Stoneman's Raid*, 83.
26. *War of Rebellion*, series I, vol. 49, part I, 335; Howard, *Dark Corner Heritage*, 9–11; Lawrence, *Shadows of Hogback*, 9, 25; Barrett, *Civil War in North Carolina*, 364; Charles, *Narrative History of Union County*, 202–03; *Weekly Union Times*, 12 November 1886.
27. Ibid.
28. Ibid.
29. *War of Rebellion*, series I, vol. 49, part I, 335; Van Noppen, *Stoneman's Raid*, 82.
30. Ibid.

31. *War of Rebellion*, series I, vol. 49, part I, 335.
32. Ibid.
33. Barrett, *Civil War in North Carolina*, 364.
34. Ibid., 381–89; Bradley, *This Astounding Close*, 178–83.
35. Van Noppen, *Stoneman's Raid*, 82; *War of Rebellion*, Series I, vol. 49, Part I, 335.
36. Van Noppen, *Stoneman's Raid*, 84.
37. Ibid., 85.
38. Ibid., 84–85.
39. *War of Rebellion*, series I, vol. 49, part I, 335.
40. Van Noppen, *Stoneman's Raid*, 85.
41. Ibid.
42. Van Noppen, *Stoneman's Raid*, 89.
43. Ibid.
44. Kirk, *Fifteenth Pennsylvania*, 507.
45. Ibid.
46. Ibid.
47. Lattimore, *Across Two Centuries*, 71–72.
48. Ibid.
49. *War of Rebellion*, series I, vol. 49, part I, 331–33.
50. Barrett, *Civil War in North Carolina*, 387–89; Bradley, *This Astounding Close*, 182–83.
51. Inscoe and McKinney, *Heart of Confederate Appalachia*, 255–57; Sondley, *History of Buncombe County*, 698–99; Van Noppen, *Stoneman's Raid*, 90; Fordney, *George Stoneman*, 118; Barrett, *Civil War in North Carolina*, 364–65; *Asheville Citizen-Times*, "Century of Challenge," January 26, 1969; *Asheville Citizen-Times*, "Yankee Troops Were Plunderers, William Henry's Diary Reveals," April 7, 1965; *Asheville Citizen-Times*, "Stoneman's Raid Remains Obscure," n.d.
52. Ibid.
53. Ibid.
54. Ibid.
55. Ibid.
56. Van Noppen, *Stoneman's Raid*, 91–92.
57. Ibid.
58. Ibid.
59. Ibid.
60. Ibid.
61. Ibid.

62. Ibid., 92.
63. Ibid.
64. Ibid.
65. Ibid.
66. Ibid., 90; Fordney, *George Stoneman*, 119; Barrett, *Civil War in North Carolina*, 366.
67. Ibid.

Chapter 2

68. Kirk, *Fifteenth Pennsylvania*, 508–09.
69. Swanson, *Manhunt*, 221–23.
70. Ibid.
71. Kirk, *Fifteenth Pennsylvania*, 508–09; Swanson, *Manhunt*, 46–48, 146–47, 174–75, 221–23, 233–34, 330–31; *War of Rebellion*, series I, vol. 49, part I, 546–47.
72. Ibid.
73. *War of Rebellion*, series I, vol. 49, part I, 546–47.
74. Ibid.
75. Kirk, *Fifteenth Pennsylvania*, 509.
76. Van Noppen, *Stoneman's Raid*, 76.
77. South Carolina Division of the United Daughters of the Confederacy, *Recollections and Reminiscences*, vol. 5, 488–89 (hereafter cited as *Recollections and Reminiscences*); Ivey, *I Know What I Know*, 129.
78. *Fort Mill Times*, "Cannons in the Catawba?"; *Recollections and Reminiscences*, vol. 5, 488.
79. Ibid.; *War of Rebellion*, series I, vol. 49, part I, 336.
80. Van Noppen, *Stoneman's Raid*, 76; *Fort Mill Times*, "Cannons in the Catawba?"
81. *Fort Mill Times*, "Cannons in the Catawba?"; *Recollections and Reminiscences*, vol. 5, 488; *War of Rebellion*, series I, vol. 49, part I, 336.
82. Van Noppen, *Stoneman's Raid*, 76; *War of Rebellion*, series I, vol. 49, part I, 335.
83. Ibid.
84. Ivey, *I Know What I Know*, 129–130.
85. *Fort Mill Times*, "Cannons in the Catawba?"
86. Ibid.
87. Ivey, *I Know What I Know*, 130.

88. *Recollections and Reminiscences*, vol. 5, 488–89.
89. Ibid.
90. Ibid.
91. Ibid.
92. *Recollections and Reminiscences*, vol. 5, 488.
93. Ibid.
94. Ibid.
95. *Recollections and Reminiscences*, vol. 1, 621.
96. Ibid., 621–22.
97. Ibid., 622.
98. Ibid.
99. Ibid.
100. Ibid.
101. Ibid.
102. *Recollections and Reminiscences*, vol. 1, 623.
103. Kirk, *Fifteenth Pennsylvania*, 508–09; *War of Rebellion*, series I, vol. 49, part I, 546–47.
104. Kirk, *Fifteenth Pennsylvania*, 703.
105. Ibid.
106. Kirk, *Fifteenth Pennsylvania*, 510; *Carolina Spartan*, April 30, 1865; *Spartanburg Journal*, "General Palmer at Spartanburg," August 17, 1910; *Charleston Daily Courier*, May 4, 1865.
107. Foster, *Spartanburg*, 220–23; Racine, *Piedmont Farmer*, 372–73; Kirk, *Fifteenth Pennsylvania*, 734.
108. Ibid.
109. Kirk, *Fifteenth Pennsylvania*, 703.
110. *Recollections and Reminiscences*, vol. 12, 1, 3; vol. 9, 529–30; vol. 6, 388.
111. Ibid., vol. 12, 3.
112. Ibid.
113. Ibid., 3–4.
114. Ibid., 4.
115. Ibid., 5.
116. *War of Rebellion*, series I, vol. 53, 331; series IV, vol. 2, 771; Van Noppen, *Stoneman's Raid*, 103–04.
117. *War of Rebellion*, series I, vol. 49, part I, 550.
118. Kirk, *Fifteenth Pennsylvania*, 703.
119. *Recollections and Reminiscences*, vol. 3, 236–37.
120. Ibid., 237.
121. Ibid., 236.

122. Ibid.
123. Ibid., 237.
124. Ibid.
125. Ibid.
126. Ibid., vol.7, 32–33.
127. Huff, *Greenville*, 144; Richardson, *History of Greenville County*, 86–87; *Greenville*, 77.
128. Ibid.
129. Ibid.
130. Ibid.
131. Ibid.
132. *Anderson County, South Carolina*, 43; *Recollections and Reminiscences*, vol. 7, 33; *Edgefield Advisor*, May 17, 1865.
133. Ibid.

CHAPTER 3

134. *Anderson County, South Carolina*, vol. 4, 479; *War of Rebellion*, series I, vol. 49, 550. It should be noted that very little information, aside from hearsay and a short line in a Union dispatch, is available for this widely recognized engagement. The named participants on the Federal side are the result of sheer speculation, taking into account what regiments were in the vicinity that morning.
135. Walter, *Guns that Won the West*, 148.
136. *War of Rebellion*, series I, vol. 49, part II, 407; *Anderson County, South Carolina*, 43; Johnson, *Pursuit*, 479; *Anderson Intelligencer*, May 3, 1866.
137. Foote, *Civil War*, 1019–20.
138. Keys, "Federal Pillage of Anderson," 82; Vandiver, *Anderson County*, 244–45.
139. Stevenson, *Diary of Clarissa Adger Bowen*, 56; Vandiver, *Anderson County*, 114–15; Keys, "Federal Pillage of Anderson," 82.
140. Ibid.
141. Ibid.
142. Ibid.
143. Ibid.
144. Ibid.
145. Neuffer and Neuffer, "Names in South Carolina," 17.
146. Foster, *Spartanburg*, 221–22.

147. Ibid.
148 Vandiver, *Anderson County*, 244–45.
149. Ibid., 245; Keys, "Federal Pillage of Anderson," 82.
150. *Anderson Intelligencer*, May 3, 1866; Otter, *Anderson County*, 8–10; Taylor and Conner, *South Carolina*, 366–76; *Edgefield Advisor*, May 17, 1865; Keys, "Federal Pillage of Anderson," 80.
151. Ibid.
152. Ibid.
153. Smith et al., *Mason Smith Family Letters*, 213; Keys, "Federal Pillage of Anderson," 83.
154. Ibid.
155. Ibid.
156. Smith et al., *Mason Smith Family Letters*, 209; *Anderson Intelligencer*, May 3, 1866; Keys, "Federal Pillage of Anderson," 83.
157. Oliver, *Faithful Heart*, 67–68; Smith et al., *Mason Smith Family Letters*, 210–12; Keys, "Federal Pillage of Anderson," 83.
158. Oliver, *Faithful Heart*, 67–68.
159. Ibid., 67–68; Keys, "Federal Pillage of Anderson," 83.
160 Oliver, *Faithful Heart*, 60–63.
161. Ibid.
162. Ibid., 64.
163. Ibid., 68.
164. Ibid., 65–67.
165. Ibid., 68.
166. Ibid.
167. Ibid.
168. Ibid.
169. Smith et al., *Mason Smith Family Letters*, 210–12; *Anderson Intelligencer*, May 3, 1866; Key, "Federal Pillage of Anderson," 83; Oliver, *Faithful Heart*, 63.
170. Ibid.
171. Oliver, *Faithful Heart*, 66.
172. Van Noppen, *Stoneman's Raid*, 103–04; *War of Rebellion*, series I, vol. 49, part I, 550; Kirk, *Fifteenth Pennsylvania*, 525–27.
173. Kirk, *Fifteenth Pennsylvania*, 525–27; Keys, "Federal Pillage of Anderson," 85.
174. *War of Rebellion*, series I, vol. 49, part I, 549–50.

Chapter 4

175. Thomas, *Jefferson Davis*, 29–30; Johnson, *Pursuit*, 154–57; Basil W. Duke, "The Last Days of the Confederacy," in *Battles and Leaders of the Civil War*, vol. 4, 764–65; Davis, *Jefferson Davis*, 628–31; Davis, *Long Surrender*, 114.
176. Ibid; Gordon, *Last Confederate General*, 152–54.
177. Davis, *Jefferson Davis*, 628–31; Duke, "Last Days of the Confederacy," 764–65.
178. Ibid.
179. Ibid.
180. Ibid.
181. Ibid.
182. Ibid.
183. Ibid.
184. Ibid; Gordon *Last Confederate General*, 152–54.
185. Davis, *Jefferson Davis*, 628–31; Duke, "Last Days of the Confederacy," 764–65.
186. Ibid.
187. Gordon, *Last Confederate General*, 152–54; Davis, *Jefferson Davis*, 628–31; Duke, "Last Days of the Confederacy," 764–65; Thomas, *Jefferson Davis*, 29–30; Johnson, *Pursuit*, 154–57; Davis, *Long Surrender*, 114–15.
188. Davis, *Jefferson Davis*, 603–04; Davis, *Long Surrender*, 21–22; Johnson, *Pursuit*, 15–18.
189. Ibid.
190. Davis, *Jefferson Davis*, 606–07; Johnson, *Pursuit*, 62–64, 70–71; Davis, *Long Surrender*, 30–33.
191. Barrett, *Civil War in North Carolina*, 377–79; Davis, *Jefferson Davis*, 615; Johnson, *Pursuit*, 188–220; Davis, *Long Surrender*, 67–68.
192. Davis, *Jefferson Davis*, 618; Johnson, *Pursuit*, 123–26; Burke Davis, *Long Surrender*, 67–68, 78–79.
193. Davis, *Jefferson Davis*, 620–27; Johnson, *Pursuit*, 144–47; Davis, *Long Surrender*, 85–88, 97; Thomas, *Jefferson Davis*, 18–19.
194. Barrett, *Civil War in North Carolina*, 390–91; Davis, *Jefferson Davis*, 624–26; Johnson, *Pursuit*, 137–38, 147; Davis, *Longest Surrender*, 72.
195. Thomas, *Jefferson Davis*, 21–22; Davis, *Jefferson Davis*, 624–26; Johnson, *Pursuit*, 137–39; Davis, *Longest Surrender*, 91–94.
196. Hanna, *Flight into Oblivion*, 57–58; *War of Rebellion*, series I, vol. 47, 829–30; *Yorkville Enquirer*, October 4, 1901; Thomas, *Jefferson Davis*, 23–24, 29; Davis, *Jefferson Davis*, 627–28.

197. Thomas, *Jefferson Davis*, 29–30; Johnson, *Pursuit*, 154–57; Duke, "Last Days of the Confederacy," 764–65; Davis, *Jefferson Davis*, 628–31; Davis, *Longest Surrender*, 114; Gordon, *Last Confederate General*, 152–54.
198. *War of Rebellion*, series I, vol. 49, part 2, 1269, 1274–75, 1277–78; Thomas, *Jefferson Davis*, 36–37; Davis, *Jefferson Davis*, 633–34.
199. Van Noppen, *Stoneman's Raid*, 106; Roman, *Military Operations*, vol. 2, 670; Johnson, *Pursuit*, 167–68.
200. Duke, "Last Days of the Confederacy," 765–67.
201. Kirk, *Fifteenth Pennsylvania*, 512.
202. Ibid.
203. Ibid.
204. Ibid.
205. Ibid.
206. Ibid.
207. Kirk, *Fifteenth Pennsylvania*, 512; Johnson, *Pursuit*, 168; Davis, *Jefferson Davis*, 632–33.
208. Kirk, *Fifteenth Pennsylvania*, 512–13; Van Noppen, *Stoneman's Raid*, 107.
209. *War of Rebellion*, series I, vol. 49, part I, 550.
210. Kirk, *Fifteenth Pennsylvania*, 513.
211. Ibid., 513, 700.
212. Ibid., 734; Van Noppen, *Stoneman's Raid*, 108.
213. Ibid.
214. Kirk, *Fifteenth Pennsylvania*, 513–14, 734; Bushnog, *Last Great Stoneman Raid*, 113–14.
215. Kirk, *Fifteenth Pennsylvania*, 734.
216. Ibid., 514.
217. Van Noppen, *Stoneman's Raid*, 108–09.
218. Ibid., 109.
219. Barrett, *Civil War in North Carolina*, 307–08; Van Noppen, *Stoneman's Raid*, 109.
220. Kirk, *Fifteenth Pennsylvania*, 515–16; Van Noppen, *Stoneman's Raid*, 109.
221. Davis, *Jefferson Davis*, 635–39; Johnson, *Pursuit*, 179–81; Davis, *Longest Surrender*, 142–47.
222. Ibid.
223. Ibid.
224. Ibid.
225. Kirk, *Fifteenth Pennsylvania*, 517.
226. Ibid., 734.

Epilogue

227. Trotter, *Bushwhackers*, 303–12; Van Noppen and Van Noppen, *Western North Carolina*, 12–14.
228. Ibid.
229. Ibid.
230. Ibid.
231. Ibid.
232. Ibid.
233. Ibid.
234. Van Noppen and Van Noppen, *Western North Carolina*, 12–15.
235. Keys, "Federal Pillage of Anderson," 85; Scott and Angel, *Thirteenth Tennessee Cavalry*, 242; *War of Rebellion*, part I, vol. 49, series I, 850.
236. *War of Rebellion*, part I, vol. 49, series II, 852, 875.
237. Ibid., 852, 875, 1105.
238. Key, "Federal Pillage of Anderson," 86; Foster, *Spartanburg*, 226–27.
239. Key, "Federal Pillage of Anderson," 86.
240. *History of Tennessee*.
241. Ibid.
242. Rowland, *Encyclopedia of Mississippi History*, 528–31.
243. Ibid.
244. "Gen. William J. Palmer," 9898–9903.
245. U.S. Senate Committee on Veterans' Affairs Report, *Medal of Honor Recipients*.
246. "Gen. William J. Palmer," 9898–9903.
247. Zuczek, *Encyclopedia of the Reconstruction Era*, 400; Ryan, "Memphis Riots," 243–57; Fordney, *George Stoneman*, 123–31.
248. Fordney, *George Stoneman*, 131–41.
249. Ibid., 131–41, 142–55.
250. Ibid., 158.
251. Ibid., 156–70.
252. Ibid.
253. Ibid., 171–73.

Selected Bibliography

Books

Alley, Felix E. *Random Thoughts and the Musings of a Mountaineer*. Salisbury, NC: Rowan Printing Company, 1941.

Anderson County, South Carolina: The Things that Made It Happen. N.p.: Anderson County Library, 1995.

Andreas, A.T. *History of St. Clair County, Michigan*. Chicago: A.T. Andreas & Company, 1883.

Arthur, John Preston. *A History of Watauga County, North Carolina*. Richmond, VA: Everett Waddey Company, 1915.

———. *Western North Carolina: A History from 1730 to 1913*. Asheville, NC: Buncombe County Chapter of the Daughters of the American Revolution, 1914.

Barrett, John Gilchrist. *The Civil War in North Carolina*. Chapel Hill: University of North Carolina Press, 1963.

———. *North Carolina as a Civil War Battleground: 1861–1865*. Raleigh, NC: State Department of Archives and History, 1960.

———. *Sherman's March Through the Carolinas*. Chapel Hill: University of North Carolina Press, 1956.

Black, Colonel Robert W. *Cavalry Raids of the Civil War*. Mechanicsburg, PA: Stackpole Books, 2004.

Blackwell, Joshua Beau. *Used to be a Rough Place in Them Hills: Moonshine, the Dark Corner, and the New South*. Bloomington, IN: Author House Books, 2009.

Bradley, Mark L. *This Astounding Close: The Road to Bennett Place*. Chapel Hill: University of North Carolina Press, 2000.

Bushnog, William. *The Last Great Stoneman Raid*. Bellefontaine, OH: Pamphlet from the Regimental Reunion of the 12th Ohio Cavalry, 1910.

Casstevens, Frances H. *The Civil War and Yadkin County, North Carolina: A History*. Jefferson, NC: McFarland & Company, Inc., Publishers, 1997.

Catton, Bruce. *Grant Takes Command*. New York: Little, Brown and Company, 1968.

Charles, Allan D. *The Narrative History of Union County, South Carolina*. Spartanburg, SC: Reprint Company, 1987.

Clewell, John Henry. *History of Wachovia in North Carolina: 1752–1902*. New York: Doubleday, Page and Company, 1902.

Confederate Military History: Extended Edition. Vols. 5 & 6. N.p.: Confederate Publishing Company, 1899.

Coulter, Ellis Merton. *The Confederate States of America*. Baton Rouge: Louisiana State University Press, 1950.

Crews, C. Daniel, and Lisa D. Bailey, eds. *Records of the Moravians in North Carolina*. Vol. 12, *1856–1866*. Raleigh: Division of Archives and History, North Carolina Department of Cultural Resources, 2000.

Crist, Lynda Lasswell, Barbra J. Rozek and Kenneth H Williams, eds. *The Papers of Jefferson Davis*. Vol. 11, *September 1864–May 1865*. Baton Rouge: Louisiana State University Press, 2004.

Davis, Burke. *The Long Surrender: A Brilliantly Realized, Panoramic History of the Collapse of the Confederacy and the Personal Ordeal of Its President, Jefferson Davis*. New York: Vintage Books, 1989.

Davis, William C. *Jefferson Davis: The Man and His Hour*. Baton Rouge: Louisiana State University Press, 2001.

Dickson, Frank A. *Journeys into the Past: The Anderson Region's Heritage*. Anderson, SC: Anderson County Bicentennial Committee, 1975.

Dugger, Shepherd M. *The War Trails of the Blue Ridge*. Banner Elk, NC: self-published, 1932.

Durkin, Joseph T., ed. *John Dooley, Confederate Soldier: His War Journal*. Washington, D.C.: Georgetown University Press, 1945.

Dyer, John P. *Fighting Joe Wheeler*. Baton Rouge: University of Louisiana Press, 1941.

Early, Jubal A. *A Memoir of the Last Year of the War of Independence in the Confederate States of America*. Columbia: University of South Carolina Press, 2001.

Fear in North Carolina: The Civil War Journals and Letters of the Henry Family. Asheville, NC: Reminiscing Books, 2008.

Ferguson, Lester W. *Abbeville County: Southern Life-Styles Lost in Time.* Spartanburg, SC: Reprint Company, 1993.

FitzSimons, Frank L. *From the Banks of the Oklawaha.* 3 vols. N.p.: Golden Glow Publishing Company, 1976–79.

Foote, Shelby. *The Civil War, a Narrative: Red River to Appomattox.* New York: Random House, 1974.

Fordney, Ben Fuller. *George Stoneman: A Biography of the Union General.* Jefferson, NC: McFarland & Company, Inc., 2008.

———. *Stoneman at Chancellorsville: The Coming of Age of Union Cavalry.* Shippensburg, PA: White Mane Books, 1998.

Foster, Vernon, *Spartanburg: Facts, Reminiscences, and Folklore.* Spartanburg, SC: Reprint Company, 1998.

Freehling, William W. *The South vs. The South: How Anti-Confederate Southerners Shaped the Course of the Civil War.* Oxford, UK: Oxford University Press, 2001.

Freeman, Douglas Southhall. *Lee's Lieutenants: A Study in Command.* Vol. 3. New York: Charles Scribner's Sons, 1944.

Fries, Adelaide. *Forsyth County.* Salem, NC: self-published, 1898.

Garren, Terrell T. *Mountain Myth: Unionism in Western North Carolina.* Spartanburg, SC: Reprint Company, 2006.

Gordon, Larry. *The Last Confederate General: John C. Vaughn and His East Tennessee Cavalry.* Minneapolis, MN: Zenith Press, 2009.

Graf, Leroy P., and Ralph W. Haskins, eds. *The Papers of Andrew Johnson.* Vol. 7, *1864–1865.* Knoxville: University of Tennessee Press, 1986.

Greenville: Woven from the Past. Greenville, SC: Flour Daniel Corporation and the American Historical Press, 2000.

Hanna, A.J. *Flight into Oblivion.* Richmond, VA: Johnson Publishing Company, 1938.

Harper, G.W.F. *Reminiscences of Caldwell Count, North Carolina, in the Great War of 1861–65.* Lenoir, NC: self-published, 1913.

Hickerson, Thomas Felix. *Echoes of Happy Valley: Letters and Diaries, Family Life in the South, Civil War History.* Chapel Hill: University of North Carolina Press, 1962.

A History of Tennessee from the Earliest Times to the Present, Together with an Historical and Biographical Sketch of Carter County. Nashville, TN: Godspeed Publishing Company, 1887.

Hollingsworth, J.C. *History of Surry County.* Greensboro, NC: W.H. Fisher Company, 1935.

Howard, James A. *Dark Corner Heritage.* Gowensville, SC: Greater Gowensville Association, 1980.

Huff, Archie Vernon. *Greenville: The History of the City and County in the South Carolina Piedmont*. Columbia: University of South Carolina Press, 1995.

Inscoe, John C., and Gordon B. McKinney. *The Heart of Confederate Appalachia: Western North Carolina in the Civil War*. Chapel Hill: University of North Carolina Press, 2000.

Ivey, Miriam, ed. *I Know What I Know: Stories of the Confederate Years*. Spartanburg, SC: United Daughters of the Confederacy, Cherokee District, 2008.

Johnson, Clint. *Pursuit: The Chase, Capture, Persecution & Surprising Release of Confederate President Jefferson Davis*. Secaucus, NJ: Citadel Press, 2008.

———. *Touring the Carolinas' Civil War Sites*. Winston-Salem, NC: John F. Blair Publisher, 1996.

Johnson, Robert Underwood, and Clarence Clough Buel, eds. *Battles and Leaders of the Civil War*. New York: Century Company, 1887.

Kirk, Charles H., ed. *History of the Fifteenth Pennsylvania Volunteer Cavalry*. Philadelphia: Historical Committee of the Society of the Fifteenth Pennsylvania Cavalry, 1906.

Lattimore, Robin Spencer. *Across Two Centuries: The Lost World of Green River Plantation*. Rutherfordton, NC: Hilltop Publications, 2003.

Lawrence, James Walton, Sr. *The Shadows of Hogback*. Landrum, SC: News Leader, 1979.

Longacre, Edward G. *Mounted Raids of the Civil War*. Lincoln: University of Nebraska Press, 1994.

Mabry, Mannie Lee. *Union County Heritage*. Winston-Salem, NC: Hunter Publishing Company, 1981.

Manigault, Arthur Middleton. *A Carolinian Goes to War: The Civil War Narrative of Arthur Middleton Manigault*. Edited by R. Lockwood Tower. Columbia: University of South Carolina Press, 1983.

Mason, Frank H. *Sketches of War History, Ohio Commandery of the Military Order of the Loyal Legion of the United States*. Cincinnati, OH: Robert Clarke, 1890.

Mathews, Byron H., Jr. *The McCook-Stoneman Raid*. Philadelphia: Dorrance & Company, 1976.

Mays, Thomas D. *The Saltville Massacre*. Abilene, TX: McWhiney Foundation Press of McMurry University, 1995.

McPherson, James M. *Ordeal by Fire: The Civil War and Reconstruction*. New York: McGraw-Hill Companies, 2001.

McRay, James. *The Occupation of Asheville*. N.p.: F.A. Sondley, 1890.

Morrill, Dan L. *The Civil War in the Two Carolinas*. Mount Pleasant, SC: Nautical & Aviation Publishing Company of America, 2002.

Oliver, Robert, ed. *A Faithful Heart: The Journals of Emmala Reed, 1865 and 1866*. Columbia: University of South Carolina Press, 2004.

Otter, Richard C. *Anderson County: Twentieth Century Memories & Reflections*. Anderson, SC: Friends of the Library, 2004.

Patton, Sadie Smathers. *Sketches of Polk County History*. Spartanburg, SC: Reprint Company, 1999.

———. *The Story of Henderson County*. Spartanburg, SC: Reprint Company, 1977.

Perry, Thomas David. *The Free State of Patrick: Patrick County Virginia in the Civil War*. N.p.: Laurel Hill Publishing, 2005.

Price, George F. *Across the Continent with the Fifth Cavalry*. New York: D. Van Nostrand, 1883.

Racine, Philip N., ed. *Piedmont Farmer: The Journals of David Golightly Harris, 1855–1870*. Knoxville: University of Tennessee Press, 1990.

Recollections and Reminiscences: 1861–1865 through World War I. Vols. 1, 3, 6, 7, 9 & 12. N.p.: South Carolina Division, United Daughters of the Confederacy, 1990, 1992, 1995, 1996, 1998, 2002.

Richardson, James M. *History of Greenville County, South Carolina: Narrative and Biographical*. N.p.: Southern Historical Press, 1993.

Roberts, Brigham Henry. *The Mormon Battalion: Its History and Achievements*. Salt Lake City, UT: Desert News Press, 1919.

Roman, A. *The Military Operations of General Beauregard in the War Between the States, 1861–1865: Including a Brief Sketch and Narrative of Service in the War with* Mexico. Vol. 2. New York: Harper and Brothers, 1884.

Rowland, Dunbar, ed. *Encyclopedia of Mississippi History*. Vol. 2. Madison, WI: Selwyn A. Brant, 1907.

Scott, Samuel W., and Samuel P. Angel. *History of the Thirteenth Tennessee Volunteer Cavalry, U.S.A.* Johnson City, TN: Overmountian Press, 1987.

Sears, Stephen W. *George B. McClellan: The Young Napoleon*. New York: Ticknor and Fields, 1988.

Sherrill, William L. *Annals of Lincoln County, North Carolina: Containing Interesting and Authentic Facts of Lincoln County History through the Years 1749 to 1937*. Charlotte, NC, 1937.

Smith, Daniel E. Huger, Alice R. Smith and Arney R. Childs, eds. *Manson Smith Family Letters: 1860–1868*. Columbia: University of South Carolina Press, 1950.

Smith, Gene. *Lee and Grant: A Dual Biography*. New York: Meridian Printing, 1984.

Sondley, F.A. *A History of Buncombe County North Carolina*. Spartanburg, SC: Reprint Company, 1977.

Southern Bivouac: June 1885–May 1886, Vol. 4. Wilmington, NC: Broadfoot Publishing Company, 1993.

Spencer, Cornelia Phillips. *The Last Ninety Days of the War in North Carolina.* Chapel Hill: University of North Carolina Electronic Publication, 2005.

Starr, Stephen Z. *The Union Cavalry in the Civil War.* Vols. 1–3. Baton Rouge: Louisiana State University Press, 1979, 1981, 1985.

Stevenson, Mary, ed. *The Diary of Clarissa Adger Bowen, Ashtabula Plantation, 1865: with Excerpts from other Family Diaries and Comments by Her Granddaughter, Clarissa Walton Taylor, and Many other Accounts of the Pendleton Clemson Area, South Carolina, 1776–1865.* Pendleton, SC: Foundation for Historic Restoration in the Pendleton Area, 1973.

Swanson, James L. *Manhunt: The Twelve Day Chase for Lincoln's Killer.* New York: Harper Collins Publishers, 2006.

Taylor, Mrs. Thomas, and Sallie Enders Conner, eds. *South Carolina Women in the Confederacy.* Columbia, SC: State Company, 1903.

Thomas, Sam. *Jefferson Davis in South Carolina.* N.p: Palmetto Conservation Foundation, 1998.

Trotter, William R. *Bushwhackers: The Civil War in North Carolina, the Mountains.* Winston-Salem, NC: John F. Blair Publisher, 1988.

Tyler, Daniel. *A Concise History of the Mormon Battalion in the Mexican War, 1846–1847.* Salt Lake City, UT: self-published, 1881.

Vandiver, Louise Ayer. *Traditions and History of Anderson County.* Atlanta, GA: Ruralist Press, 1928.

Van Noppen, Ina Woestemeyer. *Stoneman's Last Raid.* Raleigh: North Carolina State College Press Shop, 1961.

Van Noppen, Ina Woestemeyer, and John J. Van Noppen. *Western North Carolina Since the Civil War.* Boone, NC: Appalachian Consortium Press, 1973.

Wallace, Irving, and Amy Wallace. *The Two: The Irresistibly Fascinating Story of the World's Most Famous Couple—The Original Siamese Twins.* New York: Bantam Books, 1979.

Walter, John. *The Guns that Won the West: Firearms of the American Frontier, 1848–1898.* London: Greenhill Books, 2006.

Watkins, Sam R. *Co. Aytch: A Side Show of the Big Show.* New York: Touchstone Books, 1997.

Wilson, Cynthia A. *Slaves in Wills, Inventories and Accounts in Patrick County, Virginia, 1791–1864.* Seattle, WA: self-published, 2003.

Woodward, C. Vann, ed. *Mary Chestnut's Civil War.* New Haven, CT: Yale University Press, 1981.

Zuczek, Richard, ed. *Encyclopedia of the Reconstruction Era: Memphis Riot (1866).* Westport, CT: Greenwood Press, 2006.

ARTICLES

Bradshaw, Harriet Ellis. "General Stoneman's Raid on Salisbury, North Carolina: A Reminiscence of April 12, 1865." Southern Historical Collection, University of North Carolina.

"Gen. William J. Palmer, A Builder of the West." *The World's Work: A History of Our Time* 15 (February 1908): 9898–9903.

Keys, Bland Thomas. "The Federal Pillage of Anderson, South Carolina: Brown's Raid." *South Carolina Historical Magazine* 76, no. 2 (Spring): 80–86.

Megargee, Louis N. "Chang and Eng Bunker." *Seen and Heard*, February 19, 1902.

Neuffer, Claude Henry and Irene Neuffer, ed. *Names in South Carolina* 11 (Winter 1964).

Ryan, James G. "The Memphis Riots of 1866: Terror in a Black Community during Reconstruction." *Journal of Negro History* 62 (1977): 243–57.

Trowbridge, Brigadier General Luther S. "The Stoneman Raid of 1865." *Cavalry Journal* 24, no 4. (Winter): 34–35.

GOVERNMENT DOCUMENTS

Civil War Centennial Commission of Tennessee. *Tennesseans in the Civil War: A Military History of Confederate and Union Units with Available Roster of Personnel.* Vols. 1 & 2. Nashville, TN: Civil War Centennial Commission, 1964.

Patrick County Probate Records, Book 4 and Book 5.

United States Senate Committee on Veterans' Affairs Report. *Medal of Honor Recipients: 1863–1978.* Washington, D.C.: Government Printing Office, 1979.

United States War Department. *The War of the Rebellion: A Compilation of the Official Records of the Union and Confederate Armies.* Washington, D.C.: Government Printing Office, 1880–1901.

NEWSPAPERS

Anderson Intelligencer [Anderson, South Carolina]

Asheville Citizen-Times [Asheville, North Carolina]

Carolina Spartan [Spartanburg, South Carolina]

Charleston Daily Courier [Charleston, South Carolina]

Daily Carolina Watchman [Salisbury, North Carolina]
Detroit Evening News [Detroit, Michigan]
Edgefield Advisor [Edgefield, South Carolina]
Fort Mill Times [Fort Mill, South Carolina]
Knoxville Whig [Knoxville, Tennessee]
Landmark [Statesville, North Carolina]
The Lyceum [Asheville, North Carolina]
Salisbury Evening Post [Salisbury, North Carolina]
Spartanburg Journal [Spartanburg, South Carolina]
Yorkville Enquirer [York, South Carolina]

Index

About the Author

As a native of the upstate of South Carolina, Joshua Beau Blackwell has long been fascinated by the unsung struggles of the impoverished in Southern Appalachia and the upland South. While a student at the College of Charleston, Blackwell drew from his own experiences growing up in the working class of the region to build a foundation for careers in both the historical and educational fields. After graduating from the College of Charleston with a bachelor of arts in history, from the University of Charleston with a master of arts in history and from Converse College in Spartanburg, South Carolina, with a master of arts in teaching, Blackwell is presently employed as a high school teacher and adjunct history professor at two local colleges.